Dedication

To Suruba Benoit, my father,
Whose love and discipline showed me
A beautiful and truly effective path to follow;
To Howell, my husband and partner in the toughest job
ever;
To Tatiana, Alex, Bob, Rocky, and Sandra;
To all of you parents out there doing the best that you
can; and
To all of you children who may one day "become" your
parents;
I dedicate this book.

Acknowledgements

This book couldn't have come to life without the contributions of family – all the Surubas, Waites, and Wechslers -- and friends. They all generously gave me their love, advice, encouragement, and valuable criticism. I thank you.

Thank you to my husband for his special contribution with the editing process.

Last but not least, I thank Deni Sinteral-Scott, my author rep at Outskirtspress for her valuable expertise, advice, support, and dedication to this book project.

Table of Contents

UNKNOWN POET

The First Parent
(Author: Unknown)

Whenever your children are trying your patience,
you can take refuge from the thought that even
God's omnipotence did not extend to his children.
After creating heaven and earth,
God created Adam and Eve.
And the first thing God said to them was:
"Don't!"
"Don't what?" asked Adam.
"Don't eat the forbidden fruit." God said.
"No kidding? Where is it?"
Adam and Eve asked, jumping up and down excitedly.
"It's over there," said God, wondering why he
hadn't stopped after making the kangaroos.
A few minutes later, God saw the children having
an apple break. He was very angry.
"Didn't I tell you not to eat *that* fruit?" the First Parent asked.
"OOPS," Adam and Eve replied.
"Then why did you do it?" God asked in exasperation.
"I dunno," Adam and Eve simultaneously answered.

God's punishment was that Adam and Eve
should have children of their own.
The pattern was then set, and it has never changed.
However, there is a reassurance in this story.
If you have lovingly and persistently tried

to pass onto your children wisdom
and they haven't taken it,
don't be so hard on yourself.
If God had trouble handling his children,
what makes you think
it should be a piece of cake for you?

INTRODUCTION

There are no genes for good parenting. We learn to parent our children through experience and observation. There is no single how-to guide for raising responsible, considerate, and happy children. Human behavior is so complex that it would be ridiculous to even suggest that there are perfect step-by-step instructions for becoming a good parent.

Learning how to appropriately parent our child, we must come to the realization that there is no such a thing as a "perfect" parent. With all the best intentions in the world, we still wind up making mistakes. However, on a good note, we all can learn how to become what I term here an *adequate* parent, good enough to do the best that we can. Becoming an *adequate* parent involves love, courage, and constructive criticism to a child when he falters, saying no to him when and if necessary, and the ability to tolerate and "take it" when our youngster does not like us for a while. It takes energy and loads of loving patience.

Parenting is the toughest and most challenging job on earth. It is a job that can't be put off and for which there's no pay - tangible pay that is! Yet, if handled well, it's the only job that pays back priceless rewards and brings indescribable fulfillment: our children grow up to become mature, responsible, and caring individuals capable of constructively facing life's trials and eventually becoming adequate parents themselves. As parents, we are assuming a role that is nothing less than godly.

Among all the approaches given by different specialists in the field of child-rearing, one thing remains clear: children learn best when parents teach acceptable behaviors through their own example, i.e., by *modeling*. All too often, parents expect their offspring to do what they are told while they, the parents, don't practice what they preach. Modeling, i.e., *Show Them, and They Will Follow,* is far better guidance than a long list of do's and don'ts.

As mentioned above, there is no single technique out there that can provide all the dos and don'ts of parenting that fit every family's situation, circumstances, or contexts. The good news is that this book, along with other books about child-rearing, can be used as a guide in addressing our own particular family dynamics.

The primary source for my approach to *Show Them and They Will Follow: The Art of Raising a Responsible and Happy Child*, is my own upbringing. Other sources include my firsthand experience as parent to two children of my own and my late sister's three older children; many years of research and reading in the field; and, most importantly, from discussions with fellow parents and professionals.

This book contains six chapters. The first chapter is about parents' parenting experience; the second discusses the foundation for character and self-esteem; the third, love and discipline; the fourth, effective discipline; the fifth, behavior crisis management; and the sixth discusses responsibilities, with concluding observations. Within these chapters, I alternatively use either "he" or "she" to refer to the child and often use "we" to refer to parents.

Chapter 1

~~~~~~~~~~~~

PARENTS' EXPERIENCE
"Train up a child in the way he should go:
And when he is old, he will not depart from it."
(Proverbs 22:6, King James)

~~~~~~~~~~~~

EARLY PARENTING EXPERIENCES

Although its structure has dramatically changed over the years, family remains the basic social unit in which children acquire and develop skills that help them deal with life's everyday demands. It's within the family that children learn how to relate to other human beings, how to love and be loved, how to deal with conflict, how to forgive. The resources that enable us to learn how to become adequate parents usually come from experiences we had interacting with our own parents, siblings, other family members, and the community at large.

We all remember to some extent how we related to our own parents when we were growing up. These memories usually come back in varying degrees when we ourselves become parents. Some of us finally come to understand the reasons behind our parents' actions -- and reactions. For others, parenthood intensifies old feelings of great affinity for or strong objection to their upbringing. Memories of how we were spoken to, how our parents reacted to our answers, how they dealt with conflicts, showed their feelings of joy, sorrow, pride,

1

and encouragement, vividly come back to mind.

As a child, I was one who would be termed today as "hyperactive." I always wanted to play a lot, and, I remember how I tried one trick after another to avoid doing my chores, or shall I say my "responsibilities," as my father used to put it. It became, however, quite clear to me then that I was better off -- and had more fun later -- when I first took care of those "annoying" responsibilities. When I did my chores, my father wasn't constantly interrupting or spoiling my games.

My siblings and I often complained about my father's rules or discipline, but we *knew* that there wasn't any way around it. Only later did I come to understand that when parents care enough for their child, they do what is in their child's best interest and not necessarily what "pleased" their child. This can truly and effectively be done only through love AND discipline. One doesn't effectively go without the other.

These childhood memories are, in a way, an order of nature. One cannot understand fully until it's too late. This is a lesson in and of itself: that no matter how unwanted our advice may be to our child, he nonetheless *needs* it. No matter how logical and clear some situations may be to *us*, we cannot expect our child to fully understand the reasons behind our thinking and concerns. Our child needs our advice, especially when he gets into his adolescent years when he may come to believe that he knows absolutely everything, and there is nothing else he can get from our advice. This cycle is as old as the world itself. It would be heaven on earth if our child would simply take our word for it! Let's remember that we once were children; most of us *really* come to understand our own parents only when we ourselves become parents.

Transition To Becoming A Parent

Even when a couple has been married for a number of years, it's usually when the people involved decide to have a child that they think of themselves as *starting* a family. Having a child -- biologically or through adoption -- is thereby thought of as being the beginning of a "real" family.

Usually, many of us think of our potential child fitting perfectly into *our* childless schedule. This mirage is reinforced when we see parents with small children, and the latter are at their best behaviors, like perfect angels. All those who have children, however, know that those little perfect angels don't magically turn out that way just by being fed and clothed. Behind that picture of perfect angels, there is a lot of hard work, requiring loads of loving patience, maturity, and wisdom.

Learning about child-rearing *per se* and actually raising a child are two completely different ball games. The former is mere theory, or to some extent fantasy, while the latter is the reality of what actually happens when you are raising a child. Bringing these two notions, fantasy and reality, together is, however, the skillful task that those who have children courageously undertake as they learn how to bring up a responsible child. Parents do the best that they can to be good and effective role models to their child, and *become* adequate parents.

Ideally a couple that wants to start a family would discuss and plan their approach to parenting long before their child comes into the picture. This will eventually help them to be emotionally, financially, and otherwise prepared for their responsibilities as parents. Starting a family with open eyes, so to speak, minimizes tensions, resentments, power struggles, and deadlocked situations when the baby is there and needs his parents' full attention.

Future parents needn't agree on every single point. However, they need to agree on big issues such as how many children, religion, where to live, etc. As far as religion is concerned, for instance, a good number of interfaith couples go through this process and are usually better off, or should I say *their* child is usually better off, when the big issues have been discussed before his arrival. Coming to agreement or making compromises beforehand would most likely avoid a lot of tensions and unpleasant power struggle discussions when the baby is already there. When parents agree and appropriately support each other during a parenting crisis, the hardest part is more than half resolved.

More often than not, however, couples don't plan their future in terms of the particulars of adequate parenting. That's OK too as long as the couple learns how to address their parenting responsibilities without any underlying power struggle. Power struggle and control, in many cases, are at the root of complex marital problems, ultimately leading to separation and/or divorce. Fortunately, many couples work on a team basis to solve problems that arise in the course of normal family dynamics. As a matter of fact, a relationship becomes either stronger and long-lasting or weaker and destructive according to how involved individuals approach issues and problems within their union.

Some people have such a good disposition at addressing issues in life that getting married without discussing the big issues ahead of time never comes to handicap the harmony of their married life. It's not unusual for such people to turn out to be model couples and model parents.

One of the key ingredients in becoming adequate parents is the strength of the *commitment* future parents give to their relationship, first as partners in life, and second as parents. According to the *Webster's Collegiate Dictionary*, commitment is an agreement or pledge to do something definite in the future. When there is commitment, i.e., trust and confidence in preserving a relationship, people involved have a better chance of growing individually within the union than otherwise. When couples *continuously* work at their relationship, their union becomes a dynamic, challenging, yet fulfilling experience. Raising a responsible child is not, *all the time*, the happily-ever-after thing that many of us dreamt about. It's a journey that is both hard and rewarding.

Raising a responsible child is unlike any other profession because we don't get tested or interviewed to see to it that we have all the requirements to do a good job prior to assuming the position. We realize, as time goes by, that the pay-off for raising responsible children is not either instant or short range. That's a lesson in and of itself. We cannot responsibly rush our children into becoming what they are not ready to become: independent adults at the age of fourteen, if not earlier! We, like our parents before us, have to invest time and energy in order to do this job well. There are no trial periods allowed, or starting all over again. It's a one-chance-only deal as every child has only *one* God-given childhood.

BECOMING A PARENT

Some people learn how to become adequate parents easier than others, just like some people learn to swim faster and easier than others. Being a parent is almost like any other job, except much more complex. It's about shaping the future of another human being, another life. That is no small feat!

Parents have greater influence in their child's formative years, i.e., the early and adolescent years. At this time, they need to tailor their daily activities around their child so that they can be in a position to care for him, provide him with guidance, and pass on values and ideals they cherish the most.

As mentioned earlier, new parents usually respond in three general ways to their own parents' parenting influence: either total adoption, total rejection, or somewhere in between. Each alternative has its own advantages and shortcomings. As *adult children* we may, at one time or another, consciously or unconsciously, parent our children in the manner that our parents did or *should have* done for us. We may do this regardless of whether it's appropriate or not for our own circumstances and situations as the following examples show.

Patricia wants her daughter Melissa to become a medical doctor despite Melissa's non-interest in the medical field. When Patricia was growing up, Bruce, her father didn't believe she could become anything other than a wife and mother. He laughed at her daughter when she told him that she wanted to become a medical doctor when she grew up. In fact, Bruce discouraged his daughter in every way. Patricia did get married and did all that her father wanted for her. But all along, Patricia was frustrated at not doing what *she* really wanted to do. When Melissa was born, many social changes had taken place, and the social rule of women in the workforce had changed a lot. Melissa's dream was to become an artist, a singer, which her mother belittled and discouraged anyway she could. "You were born to be a doctor," Patricia would always lecture her daughter. "You can't just be a mere singer or artist," she would spit out the words "singer" and "artist" as if they were some dirty words. After some family counseling sessions, Patricia came to realize that becoming a doctor was *her* own dream and not her daughter's. Fortunately for Melissa, her story had a happy ending. She finally got to do what she really wanted to do in her life unlike many other people in similar cases, including her own mother. Patricia was, in a way, trying to *re*-live her own childhood dreams and hopes, thereby unconsciously using her daughter to fulfill them. She didn't realize that she was being detrimental to her daughter until she and her daughter went into counseling when their interaction became more than problematic.

Shine, a movie based on a true story, is another example about a father who pushes his son to become a great pianist which is the father's ideal for success. In the process, he subjects his son to great emotional and physical abuse. Although the son becomes a first rate pianist, he nonetheless ends up with serious emotional problems for the rest of his life. These are but two examples among many about parents trying to fulfill *their* childhood unfulfilled dreams through their children.

We have to *honestly* look into our own motives when we find ourselves pushing hard for a certain extracurricular activity, a certain prestigious school for our child. Are we really doing these things for our child or for *ourselves*? The answer may often be a little of both. And that's OK, since we use our past to *guide* us in our parenting responsibilities. This self-analysis may make it clearer as to whether our specific preoccupation for our child to undertake a particular subject, or to be in a particular profession, has nothing or little to do with our child's best interest.

On one hand, those who had the blessing of having adequate parents, usually resort to the child-rearing style of their own parents. These new parents are, in general, able to approach their responsibilities with a lot less stress, anxiety, and insecurity. They are a bit more realistic about raising a child compared to new parents who didn't have any good parenting models from their own parents or primary caregivers. Some of my fellow parents stated that they often find themselves sounding exactly like their own mother or father, or any other important figure during their growing-up years, regarding some aspects of their parenting responsibility.

"Heather, eat your vegetable," and "Tom, please clean up your plate," Marci says to her daughter and son. This is exactly what Marci's own mother used to say to her a couple of decades earlier, commands which Marci passionately disliked.

I sometimes find myself sounding a lot like my father. I stress many of the things that my father stressed, even though I disliked and vehemently complained about them back then. Am I *now* grateful for it! I bet that many other parents with similar experiences are also glad that their parents did what they did. However, over-identifying with one's own parents' child-rearing techniques, in some situations, has the potential to backfire. Our circumstances, for instance, are often quite different from those of our parents. We may, therefore, become inappropriately too strict or too lax with our child(ren) given our present circumstances.

My generation in Africa where I was born and

raised, for example, grew up during a time when one could entrust one's children with people one barely knew in the community. We, as children, often walked alone to places with people who were practically strangers, but who nonetheless would see to it that we were all right. They would care for us as if we were members of their own family. It goes without saying that, in this day and age, a responsible parent can no longer be as lax as that regardless of where they live.

Another example of over-identification with one's parents' parenting style relates to dating. Insisting that one's child shouldn't date until he is ready to get married, as in the "good old days," would be unrealistic and self-defeating. This made sense for that era when the marrying age was during the teen years. Nowadays, people are getting married later and later in life, and having babies of their own well into their late thirties and even forties!

On the other hand, some of us had either parents with poor parenting skills, or for one reason or another, don't appreciate our upbringing despite our parents' best efforts. We may vow to never be *like* our own parents. Whatever reminds us of our own parents' child-rearing approach is labeled "bad" and has to be discarded. Some parents, just for the sake of not doing what their own parents did, decide not to have for instance any limits whatsoever with their own child. These parents inappropriately let their child make unilateral decisions on various aspects of his young life. Needless to say that this often can lead to foreseeable catastrophes not so far down the road. Because of the utmost desire not to be like our own parents, we usually lack the courage to accept that, at one time or another, a child can strongly dislike his parents, i.e., us. We refuse to consider any parenting approach that our own parents used, even when it makes sense.

Total adoption or total rejection of our parents' parenting style is a situation that needs careful consideration. Most importantly, no matter how we worship or hate our parents, this is *our* life now. *We* are in charge, and we can use our common sense to address our parenting situation(s). We owe it to ourselves to do what's in the best interest of our *present* family. Raising a responsible child is an ever learning, changing responsibility, and balancing act. To measure up to it, we have to invest time, loving patience, a good sense of humor, and lots of courage.

SUMMARY

Some parents have more of a natural knack for child-rearing abilities than others. Nevertheless, adequate parents are *made,* not born. Many learned how to care for a child first hand when they become parents. Others learned by watching how their aunts, uncles, older siblings, neighbors, and caregivers care for children. Most new mothers and fathers realize that it's not as complete a harmony from the start as they might have fantasized it would be when their baby arrived. Some learn that their love for their newborn is not love "at first sight," or that bonding is not instant and uneventful. Their love for their child develops rather slowly and gradually. There may also be some moments of panic with the realization that life will *never* be the same as it was before the baby came into the picture. This is quite normal, as we adjust to becoming parents. It's not unhealthy, to some degree, for parents to wish, at times, that they could go back to their childless life. And, of course, these moments are often followed by "How could I be thinking like that when this is what I wanted the most in the world? I must be a terrible parent!" These mixed feelings, up to a certain degree, are all part of *becoming* a parent.

As much as parents need to be aware of using their childhood experience in the best interests of their child, they also have to use their wisdom not to completely adopt or totally reject their parents' child-rearing approach as they start shaping and laying their child's foundation for personality and character.

Chapter 2

LAYING THE FOUNDATION FOR CHARACTER AND SELF ESTEEM

"Help us remember, O God of Love,
That we all are our children's teachers.
May the example of our lives inspire them so to live,
That their words and deeds will be acceptable to You."
(*Shabbat* Prayer)

BIRTH - PRE-ADOLESCENCE

No one can predict with certitude what kind of person a child will later become in her life. We can only use parenting approaches that have demonstrated a higher degree of success over the years to increase the likelihood of a child growing into a well-balanced, mature, and happy individual in her own right. In so doing, we are laying the foundation, shaping, and molding our child's personality and character from early on. One of the best approaches agreed on by many child-rearing experts is providing a child with a model she can emulate.

The first years of a child's life are very important for building a foundation upon which her parents' love and affection can sow the seeds for the kind of individual she will most likely become later on. Whether her parents' warmth and attention arouse in her a warm, attentive, trusting, and optimistic person, or whether her parents' inattention and non-interest arouse a detached, distant, and pessimistic individual, depends on how parents play their roles as their child's influencers, i.e., her first teachers. These fundamental traits develop for most children in their first years of life, during which time parents and primary caregivers are the most influential people. A child learns how to relate to others through them. They are the first teachers who help her learn the skills she needs for subsequent relationships and learning. The strength of this foundation depends on how we use the basic ingredient that carries us through the ups and downs of raising a responsible child: our *unconditional love* for the child.

UNCONDITIONAL LOVE

From very early on, parents convey the meaning of love through their devotion, concern, and affection for the well being of their newborn. Parents see to it that their baby eats well, sleeps well, and is in good health. Most importantly, they help their baby interact well within her environment, which at this point consists mostly of her parents. Even though it might have not been love at first sight with their child, the day to day interactions with her eventually bring about a much more profound relationship. Through these interactions, parents show the most nurturing ingredient to a healthy upbringing: *unconditional love.*

"Just love him, and everything will fall into place," our son's pediatrician once said to us when my husband and I became parents for the first time. Even with a considerable amount of child-care "training" people may get from family and friends' small children, when your own comes along, it's a completely different story.

This is the same feeling whether the baby is biological or adopted. When you know that the little bundle in your arms *completely* depends on you for her survival, it's both frightening AND exciting at the same time.

After all, what is this *unconditional love* we hear so much about? According to the *Webster's Collegiate Dictionary*, unconditional love is the commitment to support, love and respect a child. It's the determination to be, or learn to be, patient as we appropriately guide her regardless of the numerous "mistakes" or misbehavior that she does -- or that we do for that matter -- in the process of learning family and social values necessary for her *total* growth.

"Just love him, and everything will fall in place!" our pediatrician told us. Is loving all there is to it? I knew from my own upbringing, and that of family and friends' children, that the answer isn't as simple as that. Just loving our son wasn't really enough. Love conveys not only nurturing and protection, but also helping and letting a child become *her* own person: an individual who loves and depends on herself, an individual who is a responsible, productive, and happy member of her community.

From very early on, we make it clear to her, not only by words, but also through actions that we love her *always,* even when we scold her for her inappropriate behavior. As we make clear the distinction between her and her misdeed, we are actually setting her up to choose to emulate what is acceptable behavior. Children are naturally inclined to wanting very much to please their special people, i.e., their parents. She *will* repeatedly make mistakes in the process of learning appropriate behavior. Knowing that she has her parents' love and support, more often than not, she would give it her best shot.

Unconditional love therefore comes down to loving the child and providing her with the necessary and appropriate social skills for her successful adaptation to her environment. We offer her loving guidance, i.e., appropriate rules and regulations. Above all, we love, accept, and *respect* the child for who she *is*.

RESPECT

How can we respect a child while asserting our parental authority? Isn't this an oxymoron? How can this ever be feasible? Would our child take us seriously if we show respect for her "inexperienced" opinion(s)? What is the essence of respect anyway? According to the *Merriam Webster's Collegiate Dictionary*, the word *respect* means to consider someone worthy of high regard, i.e., to esteem that person.

I have yet to meet a parent who doesn't want to get respect from their child. And rightfully so. However, when we demand respect from a child, we must start by providing her with an example: by being respectful to people around us, and most importantly, to the child. Our child deserves our respect to feel that she is important to us, that she is indeed worthy of our consideration, esteem, and admiration. When we show her respect despite her mistakes as she learns appropriate behavior, we create an environment in which she will most likely develop and reinforce her self-worth/self-esteem, trust, and love.

Our child learns from *us*, from how *we* act in different situations. Whether we like it or not, she is our best copy-cat. She is a witness when we interact with other people. When we do not say "thank you," "please," "May I," and so on in our interactions with her, how can she learn polite and civil ways to address people? When we give only orders and commands, and "I want you to...now!," our child is most likely to exhibit the same manners. The same goes for gossiping and negatively criticizing her or other people. We cannot ask of her what we are not able to do ourselves.

When we *show* her how to be polite to people, especially to people from whom we don't expect anything in return, she is most likely to follow suit by being considerate and polite. This is a skill that we can learn when we put our mind to it. When, for instance, we eat out at a restaurant with our child, do we say "thank you" to a waiter who brings us our order? Do we say "please" when we ask something from people who are supposed to do whatever we ask for in the first place? Do we speak with respect to our spouse, not only when things are running smoothly, but also when we are angry or upset, or when we are arguing? We have many opportunities to be a model to our child. Before we *tell* and lecture a child on how to be polite or respectful, we must first ask ourselves whether we are doing the same *most of the time*. These are but small, daily acts that can bear fruit in the not so long run.

When we speak *with* our child, how do we address her? Are we rude and inconsiderate, or are we polite and respectful? Do we ask her questions, then don't pay attention to her answer(s)? Do we cut her off in the middle of her explanation because *we* know what she is going to say anyway? When we are communicating with her, we can learn to act as if we had all the time in the world for her because she *is* an important person regardless of how small she still is. We can show genuine interest in her stories – stories which may be pointless from our adult perspective, but incredibly important to *her*. In turn, she will most likely learn how to give us her full attention when we really need it. Let's learn to listen to what she says AND to what she *doesn't* say but can be evident through her body language.

Paraphrasing can facilitate a parent-child *tête-à-tête*. By repeating what she says when we really don't understand what she is trying to tell us, we are *ipso facto* showing her that, yes indeed, we are listening. That we *want* to listen to her. That we respect *what* she wants to communicate to us. This doesn't imply that we must do this, or even can possibly do this, *every single time* she interacts with us. It's neither realistic nor helpful. However, when we put our mind to it, we can strive to do it most of the time.

Children are keen at knowing whether we are or are not paying attention to their questions. They know when we're *really* listening to them and when not. They can also figure out if we're answering them honestly or just sending them off so that they can leave us alone. I, for one, stand guilty on this one. My children find ways to make it clear to me when I'm not paying attention to what they have to say, or to their questions. As they got older, they learned to get my attention -- when I'm spacey and repeatedly answering them with "uh uh" -- by asking sometimes questions they know would normally get a "no" for an answer. When I say "yes," they'd then either crack up laughing out loud -- and definitely catch my attention -- or they would shake my shoulder (depending on the importance of what they need or want from me).

In such situations, one of the appropriate approaches would be to acknowledge our absent-mindedness and apologize to the child. Then to listen to her if possible. If, however, we cannot give her full attention at that very moment, which in some situations we cannot, we have to promise her right then to answer or speak about what she wants to discuss later, at a specific time. We have to thank her for her patience right then and there. And when the agreed specific time arrives, we have to initiate the conversation or discussion where we left it off with our child, even if she had forgotten about it. We *are* building up our trustworthiness with her.

While we know that we cannot satisfy our child's curiosity *all the time*, we also know that the attitude that we take *vis-à-vis* her questions builds a sound foundation for parent-child trust, and above all her self-worth, i.e., self-esteem. Taking an appropriate approach to our child's questions and curiosity, as mentioned earlier, eventually prompts her to think, "I must really be very important to my parents. They pay attention to my questions. Surely, I must be asking intelligent questions!" As her queries are welcome, she would most likely readily rely on her parents as being a viable source of information to help her understand the world around her. By the same token, she develops *trust* in her parents.

Trust

Trust, which according to the *Webster's New Collegiate Dictionary* means assured reliance on the character, ability, strength, or truth of someone or something, really starts from the start, i.e., from the crib. It gets stronger or weaker as our child grows up through the years. From birth till about three or five, trust within the parent-child relationship or its lack thereof is *naturally* taking place.

In today's society where a considerable number of children live in single-parent homes, or homes in which both parents work outside of the home, children are often left under the care of non-family member caregivers. To some children, these caregivers are a blessing; they are *there* for the children when their parents are unable to do so. These children grow up to become independent and confident young people thanks to their caregivers' dedication.

Children long to trust their parents and get their trust in return. Answering a child truthfully and appropriately according to her age is a sound investment for when she goes into the turbulent years of puberty during which time everything may seem to fall apart for her. It's during the day-to-day interactions with our child, from very early on, that we establish a sound parent-child relationship based on trust and respect. This doesn't by any means imply that establishing a profound, trusting, and constructive relationship with older children is impossible. Far from it. The reality is that, it is more complicated, and whether we like it or not, we don't really *know* much about our child as she doesn't know much about us. Nonetheless, establishing a relationship with an older child may turn out to be the most fulfilling human experience for those who happen to be in this situation.

My husband and I adopted my late sister's three children when they were already into their adolescent and pre-adolescent years, when the oldest of our own two children had just turned four, and the youngest was under a year old. We had to learn, at the blink of an eye, how to carry on a conversation with older children as opposed to small ones in their toddler years. We had to do this without losing sight of how to interact with the two younger ones. We hadn't had any chance to get to know our niece and nephews as we had lived thousands of miles apart. It wasn't an ideal situation in getting to know your child. I have to give my husband a tip of a hat here. He adjusted far better than I did to the sudden change of our family situation.

Regardless of circumstances, when parents are motivated enough and put their best effort in doing what is in the best interest of the child, even a very complicated and difficult situation can turn out for the best. Love, respect, and trust are further strengthened through *appropriate honesty* in our parent-child interactions.

Appropriate Honesty

A person is said to be honest when she tends to speak the truth as she understands it. Children understand things much more than many of us seem to think. The fact of the matter is that children always sense when we are trying to hide something from them. They may even come to believe that whatever we are hiding from them is worse than it actually is. Worse yet, they may believe that *they* are the cause of the problem we're trying to hide.

"Oh well, she cannot possibly understand this situation!" or "Let's spare her this terrible news," says Brenda about her five-year-old daughter Molly when Brenda's mother became terminally ill. Brenda even stopped taking Molly to visit her "nana" until the latter passed away.

Scott tells his four-year-old son Benji not to worry about needles as he takes him to get his shots at the clinic. "You know, it doesn't really hurt if you're a tough guy!" Scott tells Benji as the nurse gets ready to give shots to Benji. Scott had a really tough time taking his son back to the clinic the next time around.

These are but a couple of examples of reasoning that we parents use to justify ourselves when we feel uncomfortable telling the truth to our child. Especially when the truth is about death, sex and related issues, or other complex and "embarrassing" facts of life. The good news is that we can always learn how to tell truth (as we understand it) and the facts of life to our child at any age. Let's start by first giving credit to our child's level of intelligence and understanding by explaining in simple terms as best as we can.

First, we have to learn not to project *our* emotions, feelings, and/or subjectivity onto the child. This is not always easy to do, especially in the heat of a situation. One of the best strategies to take is to be in check, i.e., conscious, of our own feelings when we are explaining a situation to a child. Are *we* afraid about the impending death (in Brenda and Molly's case) of a loved one? Our child is most likely to make a scene about going to the clinic and that will take -- waste -- *my* time away from work (or whatever else Benji's father, Scott, had to do); is that why we tell him that shots don't hurt to get his cooperation?

Second, it goes without saying that we cannot explain to a six year old the same way we would explain to a ten or fifteen year-old. The younger the child is, the simpler our explanation needs to be.

"Auntie Bess is getting very ill," Tricia tells her four year old son Kevin about her sister who has terminal cancer. "She doesn't speak anymore because she is very sick. No medication can cure her," she says to Kevin. Kevin, who adores his one and only aunt, looks upset.

"Let's take Auntie Bess to the hospital, mom, she

will feel better, I tell you, she will feel better," says Kevin pulling his mother's hand as they sit in the room next to the one in which a nurse is checking on Bess and giving her morphine to ease her pain. Tricia puts her son on her lap as her own eyes start welling up. Kevin is by now crying and wiping his face.

"Why mommy?" he goes on "Let's take her back to the hospital. She will feel better, you'll see..." Tricia explains to her son that there are times when even medicine cannot make people better. That's when they die, and his aunt Bess will soon die.

"It hurts that we won't be able to see her with our eyes," Tricia explains to her son. "And crying is good 'cause Auntie Bess will only live in our hearts, you know... and that hurts because we won't be able to see her."

Tricia didn't have to go through a philosophical explanation about death for Kevin to get the idea about death. Kevin most likely will adjust better to a situation like this fact of life than Molly to whom her grandmother's death was spoken behind doors.

Being honest with children doesn't mean that we have to *burden* children with our own personal problems; problems which don't directly touch their lives. This may, for instance, happen when there are arguments between parents, and each wants to attract sympathy, inappropriately, to herself or himself. This is why I stress *appropriate* honesty.

Other family problems that may be appropriate to tell a mature child, for instance, or a therapist, may not be appropriate for the younger child. Ben and Sarah had been married for almost ten years, when a marital crisis led them, or rather her, to a case of *inappropriate* honesty with their two boys, Adam and Craig, age seven and four. Their relationship was solid until they decided to bring Ben's ailing mother to live with them. It was a major change for the entire family, and particularly for Sarah, a stay-at-home mom, whose daily family dynamics with her children completely changed. Sarah was frustrated because her husband didn't seem to understand how her life had dramatically changed. She had to significantly divide her time and attention between her children and mother-in-law. The couple became estranged for quite a while, and Sarah started seriously to consider divorce. Sarah had no doubt in her mind that both their children loved both their parents very much. Ben was a great father, Sarah admitted. He also was a responsible and loving husband until their situation changed when Ben's ailing mother moved in with them. Nonetheless, Sarah felt trapped and believed that divorce was her only way out. Unfortunately, she decided to tell her children about not living with their daddy anymore. She had convinced herself that it would be in their boys' best interest to know. However, as she acknowledged later, she knew deep down that their children wouldn't have ever been prepared for such terrible news. Adam and Craig were completely devastated, to say the least. Fortunately for Sarah and Ben, they decided to get marital counseling and worked through *their* problems. It took a lot of doing on Sarah's part to reassure and apologize to her children for unnecessarily -- and unfairly -- burdening them with *her* problems *with Ben*. She learned that honesty with her children doesn't mean putting on their small shoulders problems of such magnitude when the outcome was still not a matter of fact.

As parents help their child build her character foundation through love, respect, trust, and honesty, they are at the same time setting her up to strengthening the crucial character trait: her inner feeling of self-worth that I call *magic-within* for the early years, and self-esteem for older years.

MAGIC-WITHIN / SELF-WORTH

Self-worth or *magic-within* is the feeling that a child in her early years has about herself and the place she occupies in the lives of her special people. Every child has the potential to develop this magic-within. It lies within everyone of us. For those who are religious people, this would be "divine light." For those who are not, it is either self-awareness, self-confidence, or a natural "drive." Yet not everyone is aware of it or consciously and appropriately uses it.

When a child feels good about herself and knows that she is fully accepted and loved by her parents regardless of her shortcomings, her whole view of the world at large is influenced by this notion. Her feeling of self-worth engenders later on feelings of high self-esteem about herself. Self-esteem is crucial if she is to thrive in the world beyond her family confines. School is usually her first step into the world out there. A youngster with a good sense of her self-worth has a good disposition and a good start, so to speak, in life. She is able to learn to her fullest potential.

Self-worth or magic-within doesn't just happen in a vacuum. As explained earlier, it comes with nurturing, i.e., love and trust. It takes a lot of work, tact, and loads of patience, day in and day out, to teach a child about her *magic-within*, i.e., her power. It does pay off in the long run! When our child comes to understand that even when she's had a terrible, lousy day, she *still* has her *magic-within* to eventually lift her up, she develops a spirit of tenacity and doesn't easily give up. She is able to tackle challenges with persistence and confidence. Indeed, self-worth can lead to perseverance, courage, and hope as she puts her best effort into whatever needs to be done. What some might see as a *failure*, a child who has developed her *magic-within* will learn to see as a "miss" or a *trial*, a challenge, and an opportunity to learn and do better.

Knowing that she has *magic-within*, even when she experiences setbacks, a child is able to learn how to cope better the next time around. She knows that setbacks don't occur because s*he is* stupid, even though she is naturally bound to get upset after a "failure." She learns not to be unnecessarily hard on herself. She will eventually learn that as frustrating as a "miss" can be, she is not expected or bound to do everything the right way every time. She learns that, depending on circumstances and her skills, she is likely to do better in some things than in others, and that's perfectly all right. Failure in some things doesn't make her less of a person compared to others, or she doesn't become more of a person if she does better than others in some other things. She eventually gains self-confidence and starts to rely more and more on herself.

We, parents, can foster our child's self-reliance by allowing her to play a role in our family dynamics through, for instance, daily chores and active participation during family discussions. As soon as a child is able to do something by herself, by all means, we need to let her do it, even if it takes a great deal of time and patience on our part, even if the task is not done according to *our* standards. Not only is she becoming self-reliant, but she also is affirming herself and building up her self-esteem. She is more likely to feel proud knowing that she really counts and is needed by a family that loves and respects her.

When parents are bombarded with a million and one family demands throughout the day, some of us, unfortunately, just want our child to do as told and to blindly obey rather than question us. We feel that we don't have the time or energy to explain to her the *whys* and the *wherefores* of things. Blind obedience seems a tempting option to expedite things, which it often does *albeit* in the short run. However, the downside of blind obedience is much more damaging as the child gets older: constant power struggles within parent-child interactions, lack of respect, and full blown rebellion. Some of us prefer blind obedience because we believe that, "Parents always know best," which, in many ways, we do, given our experience over the years. However, when this philosophy goes to extreme, it leads to catastrophe: we shut off our child's independent learning.

Blind obedience is also often preferred at school by some teachers, sometimes for sound reasons. However, it becomes counterproductive when teachers reward some children for blind obedience and punish others who question things they are being taught. I personally went through such an experience at an elementary school when I was repeatedly punished for asking too many questions, even though, at home, my father raised us to believe that one truly learns by asking questions and thinking for oneself.

The sooner and earlier we teach our child how to use her "thinking power," the sooner she learns how to make appropriate choices by herself and for herself. Obviously, most of her choices are *guided* when she is still in her early and adolescent years. A child who learns from early on how to think constructively for herself is more likely to resist negative peer pressure during her adolescent years. It takes lots of patience and courage to learn to allow a child to speak her own mind and make decisions.

By using her *magic-within*, she learns to differentiate between right and wrong. She develops, by the same token, a conscience. According to the *Webster's New Collegiate Dictionary*, *conscience* is the sense or consciousness of the moral goodness or blameworthiness of one's own conduct, intentions, or character together with a feeling of obligation to do right or be good. Our child may not really understand the importance and effects of her *magic-within* when she is still very young. As she grows older, she is likely to realize that she doesn't need to go looking for something *out there* to feel important, good about herself, or be happy. She has her God-given power *within*. She would eventually learn that she doesn't need her parents or caregivers to be around for her to behave appropriately. Her *power-within*, i.e., her conscience, influences her behavior. When she does do something unacceptable, what would matter most isn't her fear of being or not being caught, but rather that she *herself* knows whether or not she is truthful and honest to *herself*.

Children have a tendency to *not* think first before they jump on a bandwagon. Usually, when a child misbehaves, it is a result of failing to think *before* she acts. Teaching her to consider alternatives, i.e., think *before* she acts or reacts, is one of the challenging parenting skills that we may have a tough time learning and passing it on to our child.

When we, parents, cannot be truly honest with ourselves, we can never be what we ought to be to anyone. When we are not disciplined, or learn how to discipline ourselves, for instance, how can we adequately teach discipline to our child? A consistent, humane, and appropriate discipline style can lead to children who believe in their *magic-within* and who develop a healthy conscience (Discipline will be discussed in chapters three and four). She may eventually come to learn that being dishonest to herself is a recipe for disaster.

One day, my son Alex, daughter Tatiana, and I were talking about what had happened in school that particular day. They were, respectively, eight and five at the time. Alex spoke about a boy in his class who got a certain number of "red" pins on the board for not doing what he was supposed to do, and for talking a lot in class.

"He was *really* in trouble today, Maman. Mrs. Smith said that she was going to send him to the principal's office," my son said, looking at me.

"He couldn't keep quiet! Why's that?" I asked him as we were having a snack.

"He just couldn't stop talking, Maman. He talks all the time, even when Mrs. Smith tells him to be quiet," he said with his hands up.

"Why doesn't he stop?" asked his sister.

"I don't know," he said.

"Maybe because he doesn't think, Maman?" my daughter turned to me shaking her head.

"Yeah, he doesn't think hard," said my son. "He just doesn't think, and he is always in trouble. That's not good!"

"Why doesn't he use his *inside magic*?" I asked them both.

"Maybe he doesn't think of his magic.. maybe he doesn't know he has magic!" my daughter said with her mouth open in surprise.

"Maybe he really doesn't know... maybe his mom

or dad have to tell him about his magic," my son remarked shaking his head up and down, "and he won't get in trouble all the time!"

As parents teach their child about her *magic within*, they can also teach her, as pointed out earlier, that there will be times when it would seem that her *magic-within* doesn't work as usual, especially when she is hurt, angry, or sad. Having all her feelings is OK. It's even healthy to really feel them before her magic can take over and help her calm down. It's the same power that helps her to *appropriately* act or not act on her feelings, therefore helping her know that *she* is, everything being equal, responsible for the choices she makes and subsequent consequences.

The environment in which she is raised also plays an important role in how and what values are internalized more readily than others. Her *magic-within* becomes a *code* by which she -- or any person for that matter -- refers to when in a situation that requires moral choices to be made. A child who has adequately developed her *magic-within* is likely to respond to a problem situation less impulsively. Everything being equal, she would tend to resist her impulses and rather respond according to her internal moral code of conduct. I may be naive here, but I believe that any child born without any serious mental challenges can learn appropriate behaviors when reared in an appropriate, nurturing environment.

ENVIRONMENTAL INFLUENCE AND PERSONALITY

How well a child typically goes through a developmental stage depends, to some extent, on how well she coped with an earlier stage. As much as each child is different and has a unique innate disposition, the environment in which she dwells has a tremendous influence on what type of personality she is likely to develop. A child's first and most influential environment is, of course, her immediate, nuclear family.

The nuclear family used to be traditionally defined as a social unit composed of a husband and a wife with or without children. This definition doesn't realistically reflect the myriad variations of today's families. Despite these variations, the one thing that stays relatively constant is the desire for the majority of couples to have and rear children within their specific family arrangements. When, from a very early age, a baby's needs are met -- food, clothing, shelter, affection -- her later developmental stages are more likely to be positive. A child raised in an atmosphere of trust and mutual respect usually seeks to *appropriately* please not only her parents but also people who represent her parents, whether it be close relatives, teachers, or other caregivers. These significant people in her life are responsive to her needs. They care for her and help her build her own identity in her own right.

Family is a place where a child takes her joys and sorrows, strife and tribulations. A place that nurtures her physical as well as her emotional, intellectual, and spiritual needs. A place that sets standards on how she relates to people within and outside of it. Family is literally and figuratively her shelter from the "out there" life storms. Families can be either *interactive* or merely *structural*. A family that is *interactive* is one in which members are frequently involved with each other with a common goal of keeping the family as a cohesive unit wherein individuals rely on each other. A family is defined as being merely *structural* when members function as separate individuals, going about their own business without any real concern, communication, or cooperation with other members of the family, i.e., a group made up of *quasi*-strangers. It goes without saying that interactive family members' bonds are much stronger and long lasting than those of individuals in a simply structural family. I'll discuss here the former rather than the latter.

There is a number of alternatives that parents can learn to motivate their household to interact as connected members who rely on each other by celebrating together traditions, ceremonies, and rituals that are important to them. An example of family members interacting as a unit can be as simple as having dinner together at least two or three times a week. During such together-times, family members talk about their daily activities and events during the week. Children get much more involved in discussion when asked specific questions rather than general ones.

General question: "How was your day at school today, Adam?" Lisa asks her twelve years old son.

Most likely Adam would answer with, "Fine, O.K., or lousy." And usually that's where the conversation ends. However, a more specific question is more likely to engage Adam in talking about his day at school.

Specific question: "Where are you now with the discussion of *Romeo and Juliet* in Language Arts?" or "What happened in your first period? Isn't that math?" or yet, "Are you still studying about genetics and evolution in biology?" These specific question will more likely compel Adam to giving details about what he did at school.

With specific questions, our child is motivated in telling us what went on during her day at school. Our attitude to such discussions is also capital. We cannot pretend to be interested. She will see through it. This is also an opportunity to teach our child about her getting interested in what we do by also talking about how our day went. These interactions not only keep us tuned into our child's life, but also strengthens bonds between members. On average, a child reared in this kind of family atmosphere tends to have a higher sense of awareness about things in her environment.

Other alternatives to staying involved with our child would be going together to a house of worship once a week, for instance. Or yet, planning family activities together for weekend getaways. Notwithstanding, we also have to make our family a place where members develop their individual personalities and interests. In other words, parents need to foster activities that require the participation of all members of the family, while leaving room for individual growth, i.e., time alone.

Doing activities together as a family may not come easily. The biggest challenges are time and getting cooperation from children. And this greatly depends on how a family *communication system* works. A two-way (parent-to-child AND child-to-parent), daily conversation system allows us to most likely create an atmosphere of open and positive communication, thereby stressing values, concerns, feelings, and ideas that are important. Although there are no guarantees that an open communication style necessarily compels a child to respect and do all that *we* want her to, we would fare better when we initiate an open and *flexible* communication style with our child. Flexibility in our position allows us not only to see the situation from both sides, but it also makes it possible for us to modify our position(s) when necessary. This is a very humbling process as we admit that even parents don't have *all* the answers *all* the time. Being flexible doesn't necessarily threaten our parental authority unlike some of us may fear it would.

A child learns, in the course of family interactions, which family values, activities, and goals are most important for her family. She thereby learns the acceptable norms within her family. These norms are set by her parents and/or other immediate family members and/or caregivers. Youngsters usually imitate the way we go about dealing with daily demands, problems and conflicts as stated earlier. Do we constantly complain about our responsibilities? Are we positive or always negative in our criticism of other people and even of ourselves? Do we *listen* to what other people have to say or do we only make *our* side heard? Do we strive to find solutions when problems arise or are we only preoccupied with identifying *who* is at fault? Are we forthcoming when it comes time to recognize our own mistakes, or do we belittle our mistakes while magnifying those of other people?

Children's emulation of adults is evident in different ways. In early years, children usually express what goes around them in *play*. Play occupies an important place in a child's life. The way she plays with her toys, how she handles her dolls or toy truck, the way she speaks with her puppets, stuffed animals, and imaginary friends, is usually an imitation of how grown-ups in her immediate environment behave. Play is thus her small world where she *can* do what the big people do, whether she lives in a child-friendly or hostile environment.

Six year old Kate, a second grader, spends half of her weekdays with her mom, Dawn, and stepfather, Tim. The other half of the week, she spends at her father, Brett, and stepmother, Kimberly. Kate's parents divorced when she was about three years old. It was the first marriage for Dawn, and third for Brett. The latter had two boys, 10 and 12, from a previous marriage. Dawn noticed that Kate became resistant when it was time to go spend the weekend with her father. It may be, Dawn thought, that Kate wasn't comfortable yet with her father getting married to a new wife. Dawn noticed, however, changes in the way her daughter would play with her next door neighbor's daughter or by herself with her dolls. She would go into a strange, soft monologue when she played with her dolls. She would put her "boy" dolls' hands on her girl dolls' "genitals." Dawn decided to have a serious talk with Brett, when Kate started having trouble falling asleep after spending time at her father's. It turned out that one of Kate's half brothers started molesting Kate when she went to visit her father during the weekends. When Kate resisted going to her father, Dawn slowly got her daughter to tell her that one of her half brothers had been touching her in her private parts and had told her not to tell anyone!

Usually, a child who lives in a situation such as Kate's, or in any other abusive environment, will use play as a means to deal with her frustration, pain, anxiety, and fear. Play provides her with a venue to channel things she cannot handle in reality. The point here is that play is a very important part of a child's total development, regardless of the circumstances. When parents can afford toys that help their child expand her imagination, by all means they should get such toys for their child. However, buying all the latest toys regardless of what message the toy fosters, or buying toys as a replacement for our time with, or our love for the child, isn't in any way in our child's best emotional interest. No matter how much a child may plead that she really *needs* a certain toy, we are the mature person in this parent-child relationship, and it is up to us to make the appropriate decision(s).

Children also express themselves much more directly through *questioning*. They usually are curious about what goes on in their environment. As soon as they learn how to crawl, they go in expedition into anything and everything that attracts their attention. As soon as they learn how to talk, they constantly barrage us with questions about the *whys* and the *how comes* of things. By considering our child's questions as a door to *conscious learning*, we *are* helping her get into the world of wonders beyond imagination. She learns the dynamics of her environment and her impact in it. We can also learn a lot by taking time to see things from a child's point of view. One way to do this is simply to play with her, to *really* play *with* her. We would be in a position to find along *with* her as many alternatives as possible to a play problem situation.

A child-friendly environment does not, however, guarantee that there will be no problems in our parent-child interactions. There *will* be. The difference with a child-friendly environment is that it alleviates anxiety when a problem does arise.

As much as the immediate family influences a child's personality and character, the school that she goes to also has a significant influence on her personality-in-making, starting with the daycare where she goes. This brings us to the issue of whether to leave our small child(ren) either at home or at a daycare -- when we have a choice.

PRESCHOOL YEARS: DAYCARE VS HOME

Children under the age of three need a great deal of adult supervision and loving attention. As pointed out earlier, this is also a time when child-parent bonding sets its foundation. For various reasons, some of us decide to put our small child(ren) in daycare centers on a *full time* basis. Such an environment is usually oriented to systematic, day-long, structured activities for children. Many children, at this stage, are not ready for *structured* play with other children. They usually play by themselves or observe what others are doing so they can do the same by themselves. They often are possessive, territorial, and fight for toys with other children. Sharing isn't really a very well developed notion at this point, even though this is a good period to start teaching them the wonders of sharing.

There are some very good daycare centers that provide decent care services for babies and toddlers. For parents who do not have the alternative of staying home with their small child, it is a viable option. However, accounts of stories about abuse that goes on in some of these daycare centers are not something to ignore. Even for those facilities that have good reputations and excellent personnel, daycare centers are not a good enough substitute for a parent or primary caregiver -- no matter how much we want to believe it.

Everything being equal, being raised by one's own parents or dedicated caregivers from very early on makes a big difference in a child's later years. This is both *quantity* and *quality* time; one doesn't go without the other. A child needs adequate guidance and the feeling of a special place she has in the lives of those most important people to her before she can adequately adjust to a much larger world outside her family. This prepares her emotionally and otherwise for a better transition when she starts school and gets involved in her community activities.

School and Community

When a child goes to school and meets other children of her own age, she becomes one among many. She is no longer the center of her universe as it is at home. Not only is she not with someone who readily addresses her needs and/or problems, but she also has to compete, so to speak, with a group of other children for the teacher's time and attention. She needs to learn how to adjust and readjust to this new authority figure -- and to school rules. This is even more dramatic for a child who, for the first time, hears of such a thing as a *rule*.

For the teacher, having more than ten or twenty youngsters at the same time and asking their cooperation is more than challenging. By asking children to follow school rules and regulations, we are telling our kids that, regardless of their particular individualities, in a civilized society, we do have to be *flexible* in order to adapt and compromise to get along and eventually move ahead. To some extent, teachers rely on this cooperative and flexible nature of our child to be able to teach her.

For a number of reasons, there may, however, arise situations in which the teacher-child relationship becomes chaotic or strained. The best thing we can do as parents is to stay in regular contact with the child's teacher in particular and the school in general. In doing so, we are able to become part of the solution to our child's potential school problems. By being involved in PTA activities, in daily, weekly or monthly school activities, we are in a better position to know and address problems before they get worse. Discussing with our child, as mentioned earlier, on a daily basis about her school activities can help a great deal.

People, events, and the environment mold a child as the latter in turn shapes people, events, and the environment in which she lives. A youngster's character and identity is gradually formed, defined, and redefined. Besides her parents and primary caregivers, other people also play an influential part in the child's personality-in-the-making -- depending on how much they interact with her.

Around two or so years old, she eventually comes to realize, to her utter disappointment, that not *all* her desires can be anticipated or satisfied by her parents. It's a tragedy for her to realize that she is separate from her parents. Her first identity crisis hits her. Temper tantrums, which usually appear when a child enters into her "terrific two" years and may reappear in the puberty years, are a result of that realization which requires her to change her view about her environment and, consequently, modify her behaviors. Behavior modification doesn't just naturally or easily happen! There is resistance to change. Frustration and anxiety about this change send her into feelings of helplessness; tantrums are but a part of that bitter realization and lack of skills on how to cope with her frustrations.

Some children learn social skills easier than others. When she learns from home how to be responsible, take initiative, and cooperate with her parents and/or siblings, for instance, she is more likely to find it easier to cooperate in school with her peers and teachers. These are the skills that will help her adjust when she gets older and enters the fascinating and sometimes chaotic older years of adolescence.

OLDER YEARS: TWELVE-NINETEEN

During adolescence, our child slowly leaves childhood and begins her journey into adulthood. She is no longer a child, but not quite yet an adult. A lot of changes, physical as well as emotional and spiritual, are taking place. Some youngsters have more trouble adjusting to these changes than others. The way she starts to see herself and her place in her environment heightens during this phase; she becomes in many ways more self-conscious than before.

Physical changes that are taking place at this moment are more dramatic for some than for others. A boy may start having facial hair as well as changes of other bodily features. He may become clumsy as his bodily growth forces him to change the way he moves and how he wears his clothes. His voice gets deeper. A girl starts having her period. She develops breasts and other bodily features as well. She is, by the same token, building, molding, and remolding her personality and identity at a very fast pace. As soon as she thinks she has one growth aspect under control, another is already under way, leaving her to wonder what she should do next, or why bother at all. It may be energy consuming and, often, overwhelming for some parents to interact with our once lovely, nice, all-together child turned *quasi* stranger. Let's just try to imagine what it must be like for her! *We* know from experience that this also will pass. *She* doesn't.

Our adolescent child doesn't have yet the experience of living through this hormonally charged phase that we parents do. What she needs most is our guidance and reassurance regardless of her "I-know-everything" attitude -- as she may go on blowing responsibility after responsibility with which we entrust her. Regardless of how big she may look, she still needs our loving guidance and patience. For her, it may seem as if she is on a roller coaster that goes on forever... and *will* go on forever! She needs our reassurance that she will be OK. This is the most trying and humbling time in the life of a parent.

However trying this may be, we need to hold on to our guns and be the anchor of stability, support, reassurance, and direction to our child. As stated earlier, self-concept, whether positive or negative, in the years before adolescence usually undergoes some change. To begin with, she loses some of her childhood identity, physically and emotionally. And yet, she is not an adult! She may think of herself as already being one because of her physical appearance and the way she starts to see things. And she so much wants everyone to know and believe she *is* an adult. However, how she acts may eventually prove just how close or far to adulthood and maturity she may be. She may vehemently reject many aspects of her childhood *persona* because they are too *babyish*. However, as she matures, she may eventually reintegrate these childhood aspects into her new personality. She may realize that she doesn't have to throw away everything from her childhood to be considered as an adult.

Immediate gratification tendencies also take a front seat in her pre-logic reasoning. Whoever -- or whatever

-- tells her differently is against her, and hence a foe. Some parents want to avoid conflicting issues at all cost with their puberty-stricken youngster. From the youngster's viewpoint, the "now" situation is here to stay. She needs adult-role models to help her learn that the law of immediate gratification is not a wise one for the long haul.

This immediate gratification urge also ties in with the sexual energy she begins to experience as she most likely begins to become sexually attracted to other people. As Mother Nature dictates it, these energy changes and desires are *real* and cannot be ignored. It is more than time to initiate sex education discussions if they were never addressed before. She needs our guidance to reassure her that what she is experiencing or is about to experience is quite normal and good. There is nothing wrong with her feeling these sexual emotions. This is also an opportunity to discuss with her dating and sexual responsibilities -- discussed in chapter six.

As mentioned earlier, trust and honesty within a parent-child relationship is capital at this point of her life. She needs to be reassured that she can responsibly get control over all the intense, yet manageable emotional drives she has; that she *will* feel terrible at times, and that she *will* be OK too. She needs, more than anything else, parents or other important caregivers in her life to help her learn and come to see that the world is not such a scary place, that we are on her side.

This is a real pull-push phase in this special parent-child relation. She wants to break away from her parents. In many ways, her parents are the regulators, i.e., obstacles to many of the things she wants to do as she pleases. She wants to be her own person. Her parents are concerned that she will get hurt because of her inexperience. They want to hold on, just a little longer. As parents, we need to understand and empathize with her point of view while using our experience to help her cope with her new realities. We also need to change our perception of our adolescent daughter. She is no longer our "little girl," however hard that might be for us to accept. She is growing and needs our advice accordingly. She will always be our child. Nevertheless, we need to allow her to have the time, space, and freedom to develop the skills she needs to make her own place in this universe. We also, *alas*, have to learn to allow her to make mistakes. She may suffer from her unwise decisions. Then again, life is not void of suffering. She will learn from her bad judgment and eventually become stronger from the experience.

No doubt, adolescents nowadays face much more complex challenges than those of earlier generations. In our society today, for instance, there are so many choices to be made that a youngster is most likely bound to get overwhelmed. Family values are competing with the ever omnipresent advertisement "values." Madison Avenue pushes youngsters to believe that they will be much happier, have more fun, and have no pain if they use whatever products marketers are selling. "You are nothing until you get (i.e., buy) this or that thing!" Parents have to fight the hollowness of these advertisement values and, at the same time, they have to work even harder than their own parents ever did to transmit their own family values!

Not only are children physically entering into puberty today earlier than the preceding generations, but the dilemma is that they are not, financially or emotionally, able to lead their own lives without their parents' participation. They may mature faster physically, but they don't *yet* possess the power to decide about every facet of their lives for themselves. As stated before, with fewer families having one stay-at-home parent, many children and adolescents today don't have either of their parents *there* when they need them.

Indeed, not having a trusted, adult role model there to help in her time of crisis ever so magnifies her turmoil. And her inclination to seek out immediate gratification makes it much harder for her to cope with changes of puberty without appropriate parental guidance.

Where there has been a good and adequate parent-child relationship throughout the years, the intensity of these changes is likely to be minimal and less stressful. But where there has been a poor or non-existent parent-child relationship, the likelihood of lots of headaches and destructive rebellious acts is much higher. Unfortunately, some youngsters react to these adolescent changes and turmoil by *acting out* on their feelings. We are bound to hear plenty of "I don't care," "That's the way I feel" statements from our puberty stricken youngster. She, unfortunately, sometimes does the stupidest things. Things that she may have to live with for the rest of her life. Such an adolescent is often destructively rebellious and challenges authority at every turn. Thank Heaven not all adolescents behave or stay this way for long!

Usually, an extreme rebellious situation doesn't just happen as a complete surprise. Some parents blindly believe that "it's only a phase," when they seriously need to address this so called "passing" phase that's getting out of control. We take comfort in this *laisser-faire* attitude while, before our eyes, our child is helplessly turning into a time bomb. We may allow such extreme rebellious situations to continue for a number of reasons: parental guilt, insecurity, negligence, and downright lack of courage. "Who wants to deal with it? Who has the energy? She will be out of the house soon," Laura says about her sixteen year old daughter Chelsey.

Adolescence is the most challenging phase, emotionally, intellectually, and otherwise for both parents and children. There will be times, regardless of our well-intentioned efforts to be exemplary parents to our child, that we will be seriously challenged to the point that we cannot find the right way to deal with the annoying, irritating, illogical situations into which a child puts herself. It takes a lot of courage to stay cool and provide a balanced model to her as she boldly thinks and believes that she knows *everything*. She believes that things in life are so clear to her that she knows what course of action to take without her parents' input. Yet, her reasoning may repeatedly get her in trouble.

As stated earlier, being open, flexible, and adequately informed can prove to be reasonably effective rather than taking the attitude of *I'm-the-parent-therefore-I-know-all!* We can let our child be her own person without giving up or neglecting our responsibilities as parents, and make it possible for this life stage of our child to be interesting and a happy, memorable period in both our child's and our life.

SUMMARY

A child's early experiences at home, in preschool, or in daycare greatly influence the kind of person she may become. When she goes to school, her early experiences and learning also influence how she relates to subsequent school activities, teachers, and other people.

However, there is neither a need, nor is it healthy, to *constantly* be with our child in order to be an adequate parent, or to help her become more responsible.

With today's ever changing family life styles, the major handicap for families to interact as a unit is time, or rather the lack thereof. A growing number of families nowadays fit a *structural* rather than the *interactive* definition of a family. It takes a lot of courage, energy, and time management to find ways for family members to interact as a unit wherein love and discipline eventually provide a reliable shelter for both parents and children.

Chapter 3

ON LOVE AND DISCIPLINE

"Happy the generation where the great listen to the small,
For it follows that in such a generation the small will listen to the great."
(Hebrew Proverb)

SELF-LOVE

Good charity starts with oneself. "If you don't take care of yourself as you ought to, you cannot really care for anyone else," a wise woman once said. The same also goes for love. When we do not love ourselves, we cannot love other people appropriately. When we cannot accept ourselves, we cannot accept others for who and what they really are. When we accept ourselves as we are instead of what we *should have been*, then we are able to face our strengths as well as our shortcomings much more objectively and constructively. We are then in a position to better ourselves, to make a difference in our lives and the lives of those around us.

Becoming an adequate parent also goes along the same principle. We can never strive to become the best parent we can if we cannot objectively reflect on the way we are raising our child. When we have the courage to do this, we become better prepared to love our child for *his* sake -- not for *ours*. We are then prepared to help him become all that *he* wishes to be, given his individual potential and limitations. He needs our wisdom and loving support to guide him on the path of *his* life journey.

We communicate love for our child verbally and, most convincingly, through our actions. We hug him, kiss his booboos when he is hurt, hold him and comfort him when he's had a bad day. We strive to love him for what he is rather than for what *we* want him to be. He has his *own* unique life to live, his own emotions and feelings. In so doing, we have realistic expectations of him. We consequently are more realistic with his needs, and therefore find appropriate teaching techniques to raising a brighter child in *his* own right.

We all have good and bad moods. Good and bad days. It's a fact of life. There are times when our child will feel irritable, and we can't figure out what could be the cause. From the very early years, we can invest time and energy to learn how to teach him that as much as he wants to feel happy and good all the time, there will be times that he *will* feel down and unhappy. And that is O.K. too. It is not the end of the world every time that he feels sad, frustrated, depressed, or mad. *How* he deals with these feelings is what is important and critical.

One of the various constructive ways we can teach our youngster to deal with his emotions and feelings of frustration and unhappiness is, first of all, for us to acknowledge his feelings and validate them to him.

"That must be hurting really bad, Dana," says Paula to her three-year-old daughter who just bumped her chin against the table. Dana is holding her chin as she purses her lips up and starts to cry. "That must hurt,"

Paula says as she hold her daughter. The latter cries for a while, and then turns to speak to her mother.

"It's not hurting anymore mommy," Dana says as she lets go of her mother and wipes off her face, and heads to the family room where most of her toys are.

Validation of emotions and feelings bears fruit by using an effective two-way communication system wherein we take the time to see things from our child's point of view. This makes it possible to carry on a constructive discussion of such feelings as simple and obvious as those of Dana hurting herself against the table. When parents foster an open-communication atmosphere, their child is in a better position to discuss his frustrations, *even* his resentment toward them, the parents. This is one of the bitter-sweet facts of adequate parenting. Parents do not like to be resented or *hated* by their very own child. It's hard to take it graciously! And as hard as this may be, this is, as a matter of fact, a blessing in disguise. When we parents allow our child to talk assertively about his feelings, any feelings, even the not-so-good ones, we are setting him up to providing us with the opportunity to help him learn how to deal with such feelings.

One day Adam and Tess, brother and sister of nine and six respectively, were deciding what to eat for breakfast. Tess wanted to know if she could have a bagel for breakfast, then decided that it was not such a good idea. She would have cereal instead. Her brother was already helping himself to some cereal. He was tall enough to reach the higher shelf where some of the cereal boxes were. While in the food pantry he asked his sister what kind of cereal she wanted so that he could get it for her if it was on the top shelf.

"What are you gonna have, Tess?" he asked.

"I don't know," replied Tess. "I haven't decided yet. I don't know..."

Adam helped himself and started eating while Tess was distracted by something else. She was looking at the comics in the paper and forgot about what cereal she wanted. Ilene, their mother, asked Tess again if she had decided yet.

"I don't know," Tess again said.

"I don't know, I don't know," repeated Adam mimicking her.

"I don't like it, Adam, when you say like that," Tess said, all upset.

"So why can't you decide," said Adam, annoyed. "You always say I don't know...I don't know, and people have to wait to help you."

"I don't like the way you said it," said Tess, very upset. "Why do you have to tell me like that.... it's like you're making fun of me. I don't like it."

Usually, when they have arguments, Ilene lets them find solutions for themselves. But since this one kept on going for a while, she calmly asked Adam to change the tone he was using with his sister.

"Mommy, you too sometimes do what Adam is doing, and I don't like it," Tess said as she turned to look at her mother.

Ilene looked at her daughter, all surprised. "And I thought I was coming to your rescue!" she thought. Ilene's first instinctive reaction was to jump to her own defense. Luckily, she caught herself in time. She then asked her daughter if she would tell her again what Adam was doing that she, Ilene, was also doing and that was upsetting to Tess. Tess told her mom that she, Ilene, sometimes mimicked her by repeating what Tess said in a singing, sort-of-making-fun-of-me voice.

Ilene realized that it was true.

She first apologized and admitted to her daughter that it was wrong of her, Ilene, to do so. Then she thanked her daughter for telling and explaining it to her. Ilene then asked Adam what he thought he had to do since he had offended his sister.

"Sorry," Adam said looking at his sister.

By this point, Tess had finally made up her mind what cereal she wanted. While helping her get the cereal, Ilene made a big deal of telling her daughter what a good thing she did by telling her, Ilene, that what she was doing was hurting her daughter's feelings. Ilene then asked her daughter why she didn't tell her mother right away when she was mimicking Tess that way.

"I don't know," Tess said.

"Well, I am very sorry I did that; I apologize. And I am so proud of you for telling me that. Now, I know that what I was doing isn't a nice thing to do. I wouldn't like anyone, especially anyone who's bigger than me, to make fun of me. Thank you for telling me," Ilene went on.

"It's OK, Mommy, now you know," she said. Tess had just turned six.

We need to make it possible for our child to discuss his feelings and express them in constructive ways. As the above example shows, parents must not get defensive because they stand accused by their own child. Ilene was fortunate that her daughter Tess was able to make it clear to her that she, the mother, was not setting a good example. By mimicking her daughter, *albeit* unconsciously, Ilene was neither constructively expressing her frustration nor helping her daughter learn to make decisions. Ilene was, she admitted to herself, making fun of her daughter's indecision instead of helping her.

The above example had a happy ending since the mother fostered open communication within her household. Ilene had learned that two-way communication is crucial in helping her children constructively deal with their emotions and feelings of frustration, i.e., by articulating them.

When a child cries, for instance, it usually saddens us to realize that he is unhappy or hurt, and to watch him feel so miserable. We instinctively want him to stop crying, because deep inside his crying makes *us* also feel miserable. We may feel as if we didn't come up to our task as protective parents. That we fail him as parents. Our first instinct is likely to want him to be happy, therefore to not cry. However, we'd help him cope better when we first try to find out the reason(s), if there is any, why he is crying and look at the situation from *his* viewpoint as stated above. If, for instance, his favorite toy breaks, he gets upset and starts to cry. Even if we know that a few weeks from then, that particular toy would no longer be his favorite toy, at that very moment, it is a catastrophe for *him.* Or when his favorite toy is left behind during a two-day-trip away from home, for instance, it is the end of the world for him. Two days means *forever* for him! Let's resist rationalizing the situation to him. *We* know it is not, but *he* doesn't and has no way of grasping the idea -- no matter how obvious it is to us.

Let's learn not to force him, for our sake, to hold back his tears and emotions. As stated earlier, we need to validate his frustration(s) and reassure him that, indeed, he has a sound reason to cry. We need to teach him that it's OK to cry, and allow him to do so. Crying helps alleviate his feelings of frustration, and is as healthy as laughing. Have we forgotten what it feels like after a good cry? How that big ball in the throat eventually melts away before we can feel that quiet, calmness within and without? Allowing him to express his frustrations, i.e., cry in this instance, provides him with the skills to eventually learn how to cope more constructively in similar situations. A child, whose expressions of feelings are welcomed by his parents, usually acts out less, and when he does, he tends to do it in less destructive ways. Again, as with everything else, moderation is the key to a healthy expression of emotions or feelings. Take the following scenario.

Pam is driving her eight-year-old son Ted to his friend Seth's birthday party. As they get ready to leave, her four-year-old daughter, Cassie, starts carrying on about wanting to go along with her brother to the party.

"I understand that you want to go with your big brother to his friend's birthday party," Pam says to her now upset daughter.

"Yeah, I want to go. Ted always goes to see his friends, and I don't have any friends here anymore. My friend Thelma doesn't live here anymore. I want to go," says Cassie.

"That must make you sad not to be able to visit with your friend Thelma, eh?"

"Yeah, that's why I want to go with Ted!"

"You're not invited to your brother's party, and ... that must make you feel like crying."

"Yeah," and at this point, it's full blown dramatic crying for Cassie.

"You know what?" says Pam as she wipes off her daughter's tears. "It's OK to cry ... you are upset not to be able to go with Ted... How long do you think you want to cry, three or five minutes?"

Cassie silently shows her five fingers while crying with tears running down her cheeks. "That's OK. It's OK to cry. You have your five minutes. Then remember to let your 'calming magic' start to work after that." Pam kisses her daughter on the face and goes about doing other things. She lets her daughter cry for the length of time agreed on. When that time was about to elapse, she reminded Cassie that she had another minute or two left.

Children are different. Where one wants and actually takes more time to go through his frustrations before he can calm down, another needs less. With our son Alex, for instance, we didn't have to coach him as much about learning how to express his frustrations and get a grip on himself as we did with Tatiana, his baby sister. She took longer to calm down, and her crying was also more dramatic than her brother's. It required loads of patience on our part to let her have the time she needed to calm down, and then to reassure her. Fortunately, as she grew older, she took less and less time, and coped better with her frustrations.

A child needs to feel his emotions, talk about them, and deal with them. Only after that, is he able to learn how to let go, and to learn that it's OK to cry, be sad, or be angry. As much as there must be a time to cry, there must *also* be a time to stop crying. The earlier a child learns about this, the better he is likely to cope and constructively address his feelings of frustration.

However, when a healthy child constantly cries for no apparent reason, it may be that some of his basic needs are not being met. He may, for instance, need a little more of his parents' company and attention at different points in time. He may have something that is bothering him, but since he doesn't know how to articulate to his parents or caregivers, crying may become his venue of expressing his feelings of frustrations.

It's unwise and unproductive to want to discuss with a child about his crying when he is still agitated and upset. As annoying and excruciating as that might be, let's learn to become patient and wait until he has calmed down before discussing the reason(s) for his being upset. He cannot learn anything when he is all wound up, upset, and crying. With constant and consistent repetitive help on how to handle himself during such times, you'd be surprised how a child can learn to constructively deal with frustrations as intense as anger, for instance.

ANGER

Anger is as much a part of life as joy is. Sooner or later, our child *will* experience it. Anger can be a very frightening thing to a child when it hits him. He will eventually learn how to handle it most effectively by observing his parents, close relatives, and those who interact with him on a regular basis. If we are inclined to reacting, most of the time, with angry outbursts, our child is more likely to do the same.

Feelings of anger are usually overwhelming. In general, people don't like this feeling, and like even less dealing with it. However, when we don't like to deal with anger and try to avoid it by all means, our child is also more likely to do the same. Anger, like any other emotion, is bound to show up, one way or the other. In the long run, such a stifled up emotion catches up with us, usually blowing up in some unhealthy way(s). Anger can be expressed, for instance, through body language, i.e., not talking, but sulking with smirks on the face. The manner in which we address our frustrations, especially about *what* our child does or says, is the most effective example we can provide him.

When we try to avoid getting a child angry, or ourselves for that matter, the problem actually gets worse instead of better. One of the best ways to deal with anger, as mentioned earlier, is to talk about what frustrates us, without either belittling or accusing other people. Stating how one feels, addressing the *problem* or issue instead of attacking other people's personalities, for instance, is an effective way to address anger. Home is the best place for a child to learn how to constructively address this overwhelming feeling of anger.

In general, anger results from ongoing frustration. We can never fully satisfy *all* of our child's demands *all* the time. It is impossible. As a matter of fact, it is even counterproductive to try to satisfy *all* his demands. He *will* therefore get frustrated and eventually get angry with us. Allowing our child to feel his emotions doesn't imply that he, *ipso facto*, has a green light to *act on* them. People may have no choice in how they feel, but how they act on their feelings is in their hands.

We live in an era in which "feeling" has become almost synonymous with "guide" for behavior! A growing number of children, especially the hormonally challenged ones, i.e., adolescents, believe acting out on their feelings is the best way to deal with their frustrations. A normal, healthy kid just does not suddenly decide one day to take a rifle and go out on a shooting rampage, because he "feels like it!" This is usually a desperate manifestation of some problems that started a long time before but were never addressed. Avoidance of problems is but one of the factors that may lead a child to the sociopath boardwalk. Children need not only clothes and food, they also need, above all, direction.

Parents have the dual role of guiding and empathizing with their child. We are the parent and, hopefully, *mature* adult. And, therefore, we need to address our child's acting out behavior even at the risk of his disliking or *hating* us. This parenting responsibility is even more so important and crucial during the turbulent years of adolescence.

PARENT-ADOLESCENT CONFLICT / LOVE-HATE RELATIONSHIP

No one wants a conflict. It usually brings about intense reactions that require a great deal of emotional energy. Many of us parents hope and wish not to get into such situations with loved ones, especially with our own child. Conflict with loved ones brings about a very unpleasant feeling. Notwithstanding, when people live together, conflict is inevitable; even with one's own child. That's another reality of life. Trying to avoid it at all costs is neither healthy nor beneficial in the long, or even in the short run. As a matter of fact, when conflict is avoided, there is an underlying feeling that the bond between family members is but a very fragile and superficial one. Members are afraid to confront the issue lest this bond will be broken forever. Unfortunately, in many cases when we raise children by avoiding conflicts at all cost, the first time we try to address conflicting issues, the worse usually comes to be: the bond is broken! Family members don't speak to each other anymore and, worse, relatives even kill each other!

When a child, especially an older child, is out of

line, it's not easy to stay calm and teach him what is and what is not acceptable. Especially when we think that he intends to infuriate and drive us crazy! We get angry and let our anger take over. We become inconsistent. Unfortunately, anger or inconsistency cannot be useful to our youngster. We can learn to use that energy to effectively turn our child's crises into learning moments.

Anger as well as love are both natural, intense emotions. Therefore, the parent-child relationship, or any other relationship for that matter, is bound to have its ups as well as its downs. Using abusive language or lashing out physically is not a constructive way to address our frustrations with our adolescent child's behavior. Violent outbursts can only make things worse. Angry outbursts do not lead to calmness, but rather to more angry feelings, more angry outbursts, and so on. This in turn usually leads to the feeling of insecurity within us and the child. We are our child's role model(s) on how to deal with intense emotions. We can learn how to manage our frustration and anger, not only for our child's sake, but also for our own sake. As he arrives at a critical stage of his life, his interactions with his parents also become critical. His immediate gratification tendencies put him into conflict with his parents more so than in his earlier years.

Being the adults that we are, we need to stay calm, no matter what. The reality is that we cannot stay calm, *all the time*, when a crisis happens. And that's OK. But for issues and/or crises that really matter, we greatly benefit by learning to keep calm. As feelings of anger are high, reason tends to desert our mind. Angry outbursts are counterproductive when we feel challenged by our adolescent. One of the effective approaches would be to try to get in touch with and be aware of our own feelings. When we *acknowledge our state of mind*, our feelings of anger do not necessarily lead us into angry reactions.

As our young adolescent builds up his identity, it is crucial to provide him with a stable and consistent role model in his parent(s). It's OK for an adolescent child to emotionally shift from one mood to another. It becomes counterproductive and confusing to the child if we also shift along. How will he learn to become steady if we shift along with his every mood swing? When parents let their emotions of the moment get hold of them, they lose not only their child's respect but also their own self-respect. When we inappropriately give in to a young person's temper rages, tantrums, or bad mood swings, he may come to understand that such reactions neutralize authority, and doing the right thing depends only on how you feel.

If it gets to the point that our raging adolescent child calls us names, as hard as this may be, as adults, we can learn how to get out of the situation with dignity, thereby setting an example for him. In a matter of fact way, we can simply tell him that we cannot discuss the situation with him until he is -- and we are -- calm and collected. And not an *iota* of time before that! We may state it clearly, by words and non-verbal cues, that as much as his anger may be genuine, we cannot condone his bad manners. This may even further his anger and bad behavior toward us. We need to just hang in there and get hold of our own emotions, however trying the situation may get. We can either go to another room, take a walk, or go do some work in the backyard, and hence put some temporary distance between our child and us -- and think better about the situation and about a constructive course of action to take. This distancing for instance, may enable us to hold on steady and provide our *unbalanced* child a long lasting emotional center of meaning and values. At the same time, we can learn how to be flexible in our position by considering our youngster's new concepts, ideas, and opinions.

In order to make an adolescent child see the logic behind some situations, we sometimes engage in battles that are not worth it. Let's remember that we are not engaged in a win-lose game, i.e., a power struggle vendetta. If we want our child to consider or even accept our point of view when it really matters, let's learn to create a win-win atmosphere. Let the child sometimes win in some situations and keep his own perspective on things. Parents may find that conflict resolution through compromise is a much more effective and appropriate technique for adolescents than with younger ones. My husband and I learned this through a crash course with our niece and nephews.

Compromise conflict resolution fosters logical thinking rather than imposing viewpoints as a matter of fact. Parents are therefore asking a child to give *his* input in their search for a mutually acceptable solution. It is much more effective when implemented progressively and appropriately from a very young age. It takes a lot of practice to master conflict resolution skills. The spirit of mutual trust and consistency are key to making this technique effective.

Every misbehavior needn't turn into a crisis. As pointed out earlier, we must learn to sometimes let go of some of the annoying things that our child does. We must learn, as the saying goes, to pick our battles lest we handicap our child and foster a not-so-healthy parent-child relationship. Let's remember to have just a pleasant talk with our child. Let's laugh with him, let's dance with him. As in the business world, the best leader is the one who knows when to take the back seat and follow. Above all, let's learn *from* him, and let him be his own person.

LETTING GO!

It is not naturally easy to just let go of your child. He depended on us by seeking our full participation in his life and considered us the most important persons in his life. We feel that we are being relegated to the back seat of his activities in which we were once very much involved. Our child is slipping away from us! We become engaged in a pull-push type of relationship, so to speak, with our child. The tighter we try to hold on to him, the more painful, the harsher this inevitable separation is likely to be. Mother Nature programs it so, whether we like it or not. To some extent, the way we let go of our child may determine what kind of relationship we will have later on with our adult child. Will our grip on him be so tight in our desire to be *the* important people in his life to the point that he feels suffocated and would rather not have us *at all* in his life? Are we so dead-set in our desire to hold on to him that we become disruptive to his own life as a husband and/or parent? Do we want to run his life just because "we know best" or because *we gave* him life?

When our adolescent child is slowly breaking away from us, we can learn to be confident enough to allow this to naturally happen. We've helped him through the years develop *his* basic characteristics, traits, and moral values, that he needs to live well his life without our constant interference. This separation phase ought to be a sign that, indeed, we did come up to our parenting responsibility. Yes, there will be times that we wish we can magically change our grown-up child into the younger one he once was. However Mother Nature, again, has her own ways. Instead, we can learn, when he seeks our advice, to provide him with the benefits of our own life experiences.

Even though his instinctive reaction to act out on his feelings is high, we need to find the courage to insist that he do the right thing. Our very own examples in doing the right thing are much more convincing than the best lecture in the world. We can effectively influence our child in many different ways through appropriate directives, i.e., discipline.

DISCIPLINE / SELF-REGULATION

According to the *Webster Collegiate Dictionary*, the word *discipline* comes from two Latin words: *disciplus*, which means pupil or follower, and *discere*, which means to learn. Therefore, discipline is the devotion of a disciple toward his or her learning, i.e., following the teachings of a leader. This is not what most people think of the word "discipline." Discipline is usually equated with *punishment.* Some parents stay away from it since it is perceived as a negative way of raising children.

Discipline involves not only learning, but also teaching, training, correcting, and leading. And yes, to be effective, it also includes punishment, or the way I prefer to call it, *penalty*, for misbehavior. The ultimate, long range goal for discipline is not just discipline *per se*, but rather *self-discipline*, i.e., self-regulation. We teach, guide, encourage, and help a child develop inner discipline, i.e., self-direction, self-analysis to be able to regulate himself without the external control of his parents' constant supervision. Through discipline we are able to effectively help a child develop appropriate social skills, and eventually reach his full potential, physically, emotionally, intellectually, and spiritually.

The way a child feels about himself also significantly depends on how he is disciplined. There are various types of discipline. On the discipline approach spectrum below, I group these types in three broad categories. *Strict authoritarian* and *complete permissive / total leniency* are on the opposite ends of the spectrum, and a number of *mixed* styles are in between.

Discipline Approach Spectrum

Authoritarian	Mixed	Totally Permissive

├────────────────────┼────────────────────┤

Restrictive --	Flexibility	Lax
Nothing goes --		*Anything goes*
Exhaustive list of	Within rules &	No rules or
rules & regulations	regulations	regulations

© *Suruba I. Wechsler*

On one hand, the *Totally Permissive Style* is one in which anything and everything goes. The child is usually the captain of his family boat, so to speak. He expresses and addresses his feelings, for instance, in whatever way he sees fit. Parents using this style genuinely believe that their child knows best. In staying completely hands-off, they believe their child would do what is in *his* best interest, and therefore be a happier person in his own right.

The *Authoritarian Discipline Style*, on the other hand, is one in which nothing goes. Parents aim to get complete control of how their child behaves. They believe that, given their life experiences, they know everything, and their child knows nothing. Their child's viewpoint is of no importance since he has no or, at best, a limited life experience. Parents using this approach often have such tight control over their child's behavior to the point that they behave as if even their love for their child depends on his doing everything as told. Extreme totalitarian parents are usually overbearing, controlling, and bossy. They usually never admit their mistakes or apologize to their child when they are unfair to him or are themselves out of line.

The *Mixed Discipline Style* myriad in between the two extreme approaches is a combination of authoritarian and permissive techniques in varying degrees. My husband and I, for instance, lean more toward a mixed discipline style although there is a difference between us. I believe this is usually the case for many other parents within this mixed discipline style. While my husband leans more toward the mixed-lax style, I lean more toward the mixed-authoritarian one for issues such as politeness, child's dress code, and cleanness in a child's bedroom.

There is no right or wrong discipline style *per se*. Every style has its benefits and pitfalls. Is the approach leaning toward the authoritarian style better than the one leaning toward the permissive, or vice versa? Or is the total permissive style better than the total authoritarian? Again, there is no right or wrong answer. All depends on many factors within a chosen discipline style, the unique situation, contexts, circumstances of each family, and above all the personality and particulars of each individual child and family dynamics.

On one hand, any parenting approach used with *positive* reinforcement methods such as praising, rewarding, and friendly persuasion, has a higher chance of motivating the child to learn how to do the right thing or emulate the appropriate behavior. Parents teach their child acceptable behaviors through persuasion while providing him with loving support, acceptance, and respect regardless of what discipline style they mostly use. With this approach, we treat the child as an *ally* rather than an enemy or *adversary*. We create a *win-win* atmosphere. We treat the youngster with compassion and understanding. We convey to him that we are on *his* side rather than against him.

Even when they lean toward one parenting style, many parents use now and then techniques of other parenting styles, thereby allowing *flexibility* in the way they raise their child. Rigidity within any parenting style almost always leads to catastrophe. A caveat here is not to confuse flexibility and *inconsistency*. Flexibility is the change in one's stance when there is new information or evidence that makes our initial position unreasonable in addressing a particular situation. Inconsistency is when one changes one's position according to the whims of the moment.

Parents can have high standards for their child as far as politeness, personal hygiene and appearance, chores around the house, and schoolwork, for instance, are concerned. They can be very strict AND loving at the same time. A child raised in such a situation does not necessarily turn out to be an uptight, bone-head individual. A great number of children raised with high standards grow up expecting high standards of themselves without any detrimental psychological problems of any significance.

On the other hand, any parenting approach used with *negative* reinforcement methods such as shaming, unfair and inhumane penalties, and inflexibility in the parents' viewpoints most often creates serious problems which can hinder a child's healthy growth and parent-child interactions. A negative approach often involves coercing the child, physically or psychologically, into adopting acceptable behaviors. Parents constantly belittle, ridicule, threaten, or even insult the child in the hope that he would be motivated to do as told in order to avoid humiliations. We frequently use sarcasm when interacting with our child. More often, we engage in a tug-of-war, *I-win-you-lose* approach to problem situations. When he misbehaves, we proceed to disapprove *everything* about him. We do not treat him as an important human being worthy of our respect when he doesn't do as he is told or makes mistakes. The child is often overwhelmed with fear, shame, anxiety, guilt, and feelings of inadequacy.

With this negative and fear motivation style, we believe that our child cannot be trusted to do the right thing on his own. Motivation to do good is believed not to come from within since the child, or people in general, do not have good intentions in the first place! In a number of instances, for a child raised in this atmosphere of distrust and suspicion, the worst usually comes to be. He does not do the right thing *unless* constantly nagged, berated, threatened, or bribed. The child is afraid to start anything lest he messes up and is ridiculed.

Fear may more often lead a child to believe that fear is the way to control and interact with loved ones. Such a child may be obedient when he is small. As he gets older, he most likely either rebels or becomes pathetically submissive. Teaching by shaming may actually bring instant results, *albeit* ephemeral. Depending on the degree to which the child was subjected to this negative reinforcement approach, this may lead to lifelong, psychological setbacks on self-worth and self esteem.

In the project complex where Beth, a mother of three, grew up, a great number of parents very often used to shame their children for wetting their beds. Some even went to the extent of bringing out their child's soiled blankets to show to their child's friends in the hope that shame would motivate him to stop wetting his bed. The result was often immediate. The child didn't wet his bed anymore or didn't wet it as often. Keith, Beth's big brother, was subjected to such treatment when he was growing up. He was so scared of being ridiculed that he often forced himself either not to sleep soundly or not to drink any water at all in the evening. Keith, now in his early sixties, struggled most his life with feelings of inadequacy and low self-esteem. He came around to having a stable life when his fourth wife convinced him that they needed to seek professional help as problems started piling up and divorce seemed imminent. Keith eventually got appropriate help in regards to his childhood problems and started gradually to view his life from a different perspective. He made huge efforts to become a good husband and also a sensitive father, not only to his son with his current wife, but he also started to get involved -- constructively -- with his two daughters from his previous marriage.

The point that Keith's father, Antonio, was missing was that the child was not *willingly* wetting his bed just to spite them. Wetting his bed was only a symptom. What were the reasons why their child, old enough not to pee in his bed, did so? Could the child be under stress and anxiety? Attention seeking? Disease? Fear of the dark? In the example above, Beth, whose parents divorced right after she was born, and she and her brother Keith were raised by her mother, said that she came to empathize with one of her children, as she, like her brother, also came to often wet her bed. She said that she didn't like having her blankets soiled when she woke up in the morning. She dreaded every morning to the point that she would force herself to wake up many times during the night. Fortunately for Beth, her mother didn't treat her like their father had treated her brother, Keith. After the divorce, Beth's mother moved with her two children to another apartment complex. She took Beth to the bathroom at night, without complaint or negative remarks, whenever Beth needed to go. Beth's mother knew that her daughter was afraid of the dark and the creepy noise in the hallway to the common apartment complex bathrooms.

One of the reasons some parents use shaming may be that they themselves -- as in the case of Antonio, Keith and Beth's father -- were raised in this atmosphere. They themselves grow up to be convinced of the ever constant evil motivation within man. Fortunately, the good news is that this outlook on parenting can be modified by a personal, conscious decision to break the cycle, i.e., learning appropriate parenting skills through seminars, family counseling, or discussions with other parents.

To go back to Beth again, one of Beth and Dan's children was still wetting his bed, almost every other day of the week, at the age of ten. Brian, the ten year old, was adopted from a foster home in their city the year that the oldest of Beth and Dan's two daughters had turned four. It was, Beth said, not a pleasant situation to deal with, especially when their oldest, four year old daughter was not wetting her bed. Beth and her husband took their son Brian first to a pediatrician to see if he had any medical reason for it. Fortunately, there was none. They decided then to sit down with Brian and talk about the situation. Beth and Dan wanted to make it crystal clear that they were there to help him address the situation, and that he must rest assured that he would get all their support. And that there was no one to tease him any longer about wetting his bed like he was used to in the foster home. However, Beth and Dan told him that he, Brian, would take responsibility for his own soiled blankets as soon as he realized in the morning that he had had an accident. He would soak them in soapy water before he went to school and wash them as soon as he came back home. If it happened on the weekends, he would clean them immediately in the morning. Beth and Dan wanted him to be accountable for his situation.

It took Brian a while to get used to the routine, and a lot of patience from Beth, who was a stay-home mother, to remind him about cleaning them, day in and day out until he got it. He finally got over his problem -- without being subjected to any more shame -- after a couple of years. And all the while Brian learned to take responsibility for his own problems while receiving support from the rest of the family.

Where one family has been successful in raising a responsible child using a certain parenting approach style, another might fail using the exact same methods and techniques. It's therefore only *partly* true that a child's behavior is a reflection of what kind of parents he has. As conscientious and motivated as parents can be, they can not possibly influence *every single* facet of the total child. Parents are only human; they make mistakes regardless of their best intentions. However, they become more effective as adequate parents when they keep in mind that whatever type of parenting style they mostly use, they have to learn to be flexible given the context, timing, situation, and the particulars of each individual child, and, above all, learn to use the appropriate balance of love and discipline.

LOVE AND DISCIPLINE

Regardless of what kind of parenting approach one uses, the basic ingredient for good and effective discipline is *love*. Love is the ability to care about the well-being of a child through our *actions* and *words*. Words include encouragement to a child when *he* falters while trying to do the right thing, and being honest with a child when *we* falter while trying our best to come up to our parenting responsibility.

Lack of concern for a child may lead him to misbehave if he believes that is the only way to get attention. Since he feels neglected, he is, in a way, demanding the attention he needs to feel good about himself. Even negative attention is better than none. Everything being equal, a child who feels unloved usually lags way behind other children of his age in school and in many other things. When he enters adolescence, he may drop out of school since he gets tired of being reprimanded for unacceptable behavior.

When the parent-child relationship has been characterized by love, trust, appropriate discipline, support, and mutual respect, a child who lives in this atmosphere usually tends to be loving and respectful in return. He wants to become like his parents -- or other significant figures in his life -- when he grows up. He is proud to please his parents since he knows that his parents are on *his* side. He thinks that his parents really care, that he really matters to them. He develops over the years a sense of inner value, self-worth or self-esteem.

My parents divorced when I was barely two years of age. I stayed with my father. He was a pillar of what I came to understand as "unconditional love." There was no shred of doubt in my mind about my father's love for me when I was growing up. And even more so today as I become a parent myself. What he did and how he did it spoke for itself -- at least now that I have come to fully understand. Needless to say that when I was growing up, I didn't really appreciate it. When he was home, he did not only talk about rules and responsibilities, but he also played with us, which was extremely unusual for the culture in which I grew up. He carried us on his back. We raced to him when he came home. We helped him take off his shoes and socks. He took us on family outings. As much as he stressed rules and regulations, he also stressed having a good time. Nonetheless, as said earlier, we children knew, and *I* especially knew, that his playing with us, his loving us didn't mean that we would not do our chores or take care of our responsibilities, or go around the unwritten rules. No way, no sir. His children were his world. He cared for us so deeply that he couldn't have conveyed that message without proper discipline. I, for one, was a very trying child -- I wish I knew then what it is like to be a parent -- and was punished more than any other child in the family. Yet, I never doubted my father's love for me -- it was a "given.".

In today's feel-good-no-matter-what pop psyche, many parents are *mostly* preoccupied with making their child "happy." It's a rightfully legitimate concern that parents seek happiness for their child. However, seeking a child's happiness to the point of robbing him of the benefits of your wisdom will usually lead to exactly what we try to avoid at all cost: our child's unhappiness.

One day, as I was picking up my children from school, a minivan in front of me had a sticker that read, *"Love is not enough, Put a leash on your dog if you care enough!"* How true! Indeed, love alone is not enough in our parenting responsibility. We can also learn how to teach our child to learn self-regulation, boundaries, and limits through appropriate discipline.

BOUNDARIES AND SELF-REGULATION

By nature children are curious. When a baby starts to sit by himself, around the middle of his first year, he shows an increased interest in things in his immediate environment. As soon as he is able to crawl, his curiosity takes him to different places. He grabs things within his reach and bangs them down or, more typically, puts them into his mouth. Some of these places and things are dangerous and can even be life-threatening. Therefore, we put in place the *first boundaries* to restrict his movements from places where he may harm himself, i.e., we childproof the house. Ideally, parents childproof the house long before the child starts to crawl.

As soon as he is able to talk, his intellectual curiosity becomes verbal. He asks questions about things in his environment and often talks endlessly. He constantly asks questions that usually start with *why* or *how come. Why* is in every one of his questions. "Why do we eat with forks? Why do people take baths? Why do you do this? Why do you do that?" Sometimes, if not often, he asks *why*, and then goes on to other *whys* before his parents finish explaining the previous *why(s)* and *how come(s)*. For even the most patient parent on earth, this *why* and *how-come-question* stage can be trying and energy consuming, to say the least. We can only answer our *why-question*-stage child's questions as best as we can so that he grows up knowing that he can always rely on our being interested in what he wants to learn. That he can count on us. That he can rest assured of our straightforward, truthful, and honest answer(s) which, of course, are given according to his level of understanding. We can learn to constructively help foster his curiosity by looking at his problems from *his* perspective while using our own experienced adult common sense.

On one hand, parental supervision is capital to assuring a child's safety and fostering learning in the child. We have to set necessary and appropriate boundaries. By exploring his immediate environment, and the things in it, he is not only learning about his surroundings, and how he is separate from other things and people in it, but he is also making his first steps toward his independent learning. He is instinctively affirming that *he* can find out things on his own.

On the other hand, too much supervision, i.e., over-controlling and over-scheduling a child's learning activities, takes away part of a child's natural drive to discover and learn for and by himself. Consequently, these *physical limits* or too much supervision needn't be overwhelming to the point that his curiosity is completely curtailed. Doing so often stifles imagination and the natural tendency for healthy independence of a child from his parents. Furthermore, over-supervision also robs a child of opportunities to develop his own interests, likes, and dislikes, to become his own, confident, successful, and independent self.

As a child grows older, *physical boundaries* are slowly being replaced by *abstract limits*, i.e., written or unwritten rules and regulations. House rules and regulations, for instance, help a family not only function but also interact as a cohesive unit. Rules define generally which behaviors are and which ones are not acceptable. It's unrealistic trying to come up with an exhaustive list of *do's* and *don'ts*. A more general guide is sufficient.

These limits or rules need to be as many or as few as a child can handle. When there are too many, they become overwhelming for the child, and therefore no longer helpful. Explanation of these rules is critical; to make sure that the child understands them, that he, not just his parents, understands the rewards and incentives for observing the rules, and the consequences and penalties for breaking them.

As he learns about house rules, he also learns to self-regulate. In his early years, these rules need to be repeated over and over again to allow him to learn them. It's not an easy notion for a two, three, or four year old to learn to stay in time-out for a specific period, for instance. I remember when our daughter Tatiana went into her terrific twos, she was a full blown tantrum thrower! It took a long while for her to learn about what to do during her time-out. The first few times she was to stay for a few minutes in a designated place -- which was often in a corner of our family room next to the kitchen; this way I was able to keep an eye on her while going about my other business. As soon as I left her in the corner and turned around, she was right behind me and still carrying on! I had to take her back again and again. There were times when I sat with her for a while and explained that she couldn't leave that place until her two or three minutes to calm down were up. With perseverance on my part, she eventually got it.

A child may also learn self-discipline through stories and play. Having rules and regulations creates a sense of true freedom; these rules actually provide acceptable, constructive ways for a child to channel and express his "negative" feelings, especially those of sadness, frustration, and anger. I put "negative" in quotation simply because these feelings actually can be and are positive in certain situations. When a child has been repeatedly picked on for no reason, for instance, that child has the right to be upset. It's perfectly *healthy* for a child to express these feelings. We can teach him the skills on how to talk and express his feelings in a constructive way to work out his problems rather than get physical. In so doing, he learns how to deal with emotions such as jealousy, sibling rivalry, teasing, and bullying.

Children tease each other from time to time. It's not a cause for alarm unless it becomes a regular and constant happening. When teasing becomes malicious because of sibling rivalry, for instance, we must step in. Usually, children would say that it was *only* a joke or funny. We have to make it clear that a joke is a joke when both parties are laughing. It ceases to be a joke when one is hurting or our intention is to demean the other. It becomes an insult. The teaser needs to be taught the law of reciprocity, i.e. being in another person's shoes. What and how would he feel if he were being treated as he treated his brother or sister? Eventually, the child will develop sympathy for other people's feelings.

We also have to listen to ourselves when we tell jokes to a child. Are we indirectly belittling him? Does he understand that it's a joke? He is not likely to react to our jokes as he would with his peers. Can he say back to us the same jokes without offending us? If the answer is clear to all these question, then we can either say the joke or not. We must stop any joke that a child doesn't understand or doesn't find funny. Otherwise, we may, consciously or unconsciously, be rude to or bully a child.

Many parents, including me, had experiences with bullies when they were children. When the bullying is a constant daily occurrence at school for instance, a child may and usually does lose interest in going to school. He may ultimately no longer apply himself. One of the best ways to deal with a bully is to ignore him or her completely as long as he/she doesn't engage in physical or verbal threats. However, when a youngster is constantly and regularly being bullied by an older child, there is nothing wrong with intervening on the younger child's behalf.

One day Arthur, an eight year old, came home from school and told his parents that he was choked on the school bus by another child. His parents, Lynn and Michael, had talked to Arthur about teasers and bullies, and how to handle them. Arthur knew how to ignore teasers and bullies. He usually told his parents about his days at school, and about how he felt so good when he didn't pay any attention to would-be bullies who usually didn't know what else to do when he ignored them. And how they would stop teasing him altogether and went on to pick on somebody else! Somehow another child, Craig, who was on the same school bus and much older than Arthur wasn't turned off by being ignored. He went further and became physical. Lynn and Michael asked their son how it all started and how it came to the shoving, pushing, and choking.

"He first started teasing my friend Reed," Arthur said. "And I was talking to Reed when he came and started pushing and choking my friend. I told them to stop. He then turned to me and started choking me, too. I told him to stop many times and tried to take his hands off my neck, but he kept on choking... It was hurting! When he didn't stop, I pushed him back hard and screamed again to stop! The bus driver then told him to stop."

When this incident repeated itself, and Arthur asked the bully to stop to no avail, Lynn and Michael decided to go speak with the child. They asked Craig, the eleven year old bully, to tell his side of the story. Craig kept silent. Lynn and Michael explained to him that it was wrong to bother and assault, not only Arthur, their son, but other children as well. They explained to Craig that the bullying was not acceptable behavior, and that it had to stop, *immediately*. They explained to him that they would go meet with his parents if they heard one more incident about him bothering either Arthur or any other kid on the bus. The bullying stopped. To no one's surprise, Craig had many problems at home, as Lynn and Michael later found out. He lived in what one would call a "disturbed" family atmosphere. He was obviously taking out his frustrations on other children who were younger than him.

By addressing and offering protection to their son, Lynn and Michael were asserting their role as concerned, caring, loving, and supportive parents to both their son and even, in some ways, to Craig, the bully. Fortunately for Craig, Lynn and Michael understood that, usually, children who are bullies are not really bad kids. They usually have family problems, and they take it out on those who can't physically defend themselves.

When it is our child who is the teaser or bully, as explained earlier, we need to explain to him how he would feel if he were to be teased by someone else. We also take opportunities like these - and whenever our child steps out of line -- to offer him not only constructive criticism, but also what appropriate alternatives he needs to think about when a similar situation arises again.

CRITICISM

When a child falters, which *will* happen, we are to teach him how to learn from his mistakes, and to let him know that making mistakes, in many instances, is also part of the learning process. By helping a child learn from his mistakes, parents need to first discuss what happened, the *whys* and the *hows* of the mishap. They, therefore, analyze and criticize the *situation,* not the child.

The word *criticism* usually has a negative connotation. According to the *Merriam Webster's Collegiate Dictionary*, to criticize is to evaluate, usually unfavorably. Justifiably so, a number of parents stay away from it when it comes to addressing their child's misbehavior -- or their own for that matter. However, criticism can be *positively* or *negatively* oriented.

Positive criticism is an evaluation which goal is to motivate the child to adopt an acceptable behavior. Positive criticism *evaluates* a child's misbehavior AND has a *corrective* or *motivating course of action* to help modify the misbehavior. This ultimately leads to self-discipline or self-regulation. It is about making a positive out of a minus. Example 1 is positive criticism, example 2 is not.

Example 1: "Yes, Bill, you can play with your Gameboy after you finish your homework."
Example 2: "No, you can't play with your game boy now. You always want to play instead of doing your homework. You're very irresponsible."

Positive criticism usually makes the child less defensive in addressing his misbehavior. He doesn't feel under attack. The likelihood that he would adopt acceptable behavior is high. In example 1, Bill is more likely to get down to his homework. Through positive criticism we provide him with support as he eventually learns from his mistakes.

Negative criticism does just the contrary. Its goal is *only* to censure, to reprobate, to condemn, to find faults without any corrective plan to follow. It conveys rejection of the misbehaving child as portrayed in example 2 above. Constant blame for unacceptable behavior is not a good *de*motivator for unwanted behavior.

Positive criticism also provides an opportunity to show that parents are human. In our child's eyes, we are the most powerful persons in the universe. This is the time to make it clear to him that everybody makes mistakes, even his parents! The earlier we let him know this, the more respect and compassion he may eventually have for us. When we positively criticize a child in this atmosphere of honesty, he is likely to also take our criticism constructively. He is likely to see it as a loving effort on our part to help him. During criticism we have to *not neglect* to stress the other aspects of a child's personality of which we are proud. We must tell him -- and mean it because children can easily see through -- how much we love and appreciate him, how happy and blessed we are to have him in our lives. A simple word of praise and encouragement, a hug, a pat on the back at the end or during these teaching moments, can help bring us and our child closer. We can then both address the criticized misbehavior positively.

We all want our child to be motivated enough to become successful in whatever he chooses to do. True motivation or enthusiasm really comes from *within*. We can only foster or create motivators which are likely to raise his interest, imagination, and enthusiasm. We can learn how *not* to push a child to "succeed" at all cost because *we* know what he should do to succeed. We help him even more so by giving him the freedom to fail.

When my son Alex was in his last year of elementary school, he was working on a math project; he had to build a fort. Somehow, I decided that since he had many after-school activities the day before the project was due, I would go ahead and start building his fort to "help" him. I stayed up quite late that evening working on it. The day after, my daughter Tatiana came back home from school before her brother got home. When she saw the fort, she asked me who did it. I told her that I was "helping" her brother with his homework. Her next question shamed me, to say the least: "That's Alex's homework, Maman. Are you doing his homework for him?"

When my son got home from school and saw the fort, he didn't like it! He decided to make a different one. I resisted the temptation to "help" him again -- which was not really helping him but *myself* because I wanted him to finish it fast so that I could go to sleep. I actually knew, deep down, that what I was doing was not really helping *him*. And my daughter's remarks were just the last drop that spilled water over. He finished his project fort by himself without my "help."

Even during positive criticism, a child is bound to sometimes feel sad, guilty, or upset. That is OK. Some parents don't really like to see their child feel "bad" about something that he did wrong. They expect the child to take criticism without any emotion or feeling of regret. God forbid that he should feel sad, gloomy, or even cry. Now, let me make this clear. The goal for our criticism is not to hurt the child or make him cry. That is cruelty. But, for our child's sake, let's let him go through the learning process which brings about change in his behaviors. Learning is not always easy. *Ditto* for change of behavior.

Real change is usually not easy. Parents themselves resist change, in one way or another. Why then do we believe that our child would just change his unacceptable behavior goodheartedly because we ask him to? And when he shows hurt feelings, why do we think it is necessary to stop correcting an unacceptable behavior? Unfortunately, a great number of parents prefer the "Don't judge, Don't criticize" approach whenever they are faced with their child's inappropriate behavior.

When a child seriously blows it, some parents rush to say, "It's OK, don't cry, it's OK," because they are afraid that this would supposedly break his self-esteem. These are contradictory messages to a child as a matter of fact. "Your behavior is unacceptable, but it's OK!" We must, of course, comfort our child; he definitely feels bad and concerned that his favorite people, his parents, are criticizing his inappropriate behavior. He fears that they might be rejecting him along with his misbehavior. We can learn both to comfort him AND make it clear that it's his *misbehavior*, not *him*, that is in question. Therefore, we do not only explain to him that his behavior was unacceptable, but we also lift his spirits, that he is a terrific kid who made a mistake that he is capable of correcting.

Equally important is for both parent AND child to come up with acceptable behavior alternatives to be adopted. Believe you me, children can come up with extraordinary options when we give them a chance! And if they don't, well, that's why we are the parents!

We must honestly ask ourselves, are we concerned because we feel that our parenting abilities and self-esteem as parents are put to the test? And that we are failing because our child isn't acting as he *should*? If the answer is yes, we are not doing our child a favor. We are, instead, just seeking a *quick fix* that, in reality, makes *us* feel good while we put our child's character in jeopardy. Is it too late to change a course of action if we are used to quick fix parenting approaches to motivate our child to emulate acceptable behavior? Never! Honesty and courage is what we need to start the process: being conscious of the way we go about teaching our child to be a decent and good person.

The process for learning some facts of life is not always a pleasant one. We cannot shield our child from that, no matter how much we want to if we are to raise a mentally healthy, decent, independent, compassionate, mature, and responsible child. Let's teach him -- and ourselves -- not to equate *loving* him with *liking all* that he does.

"Mommy, I don't want to go to the game with you, but I love you," said five year old Meg to Carol, her mother. She kisses her mother after the latter asks her to go along with her to see Meg's brother's game.

Carol was disappointed that her daughter didn't go with them. But she sure was proud of how her daughter expressed herself. Meg knew that her mother being disappointed and her loving her mother were two quite different things. Needless to say Carol returned her daughter's kisses tenfold before she went out of the door with Todd, her son.

SUMMARY

Social and peer pressure to conform is so high nowadays that children need strong role models from home to build strong character and high self-esteem. Youngsters who learn standards for acceptable behavior have a lower likelihood of becoming juvenile delinquents. We also have to stress appreciation for our child's efforts by accentuating the positive, and acknowledging his accomplishments however small they may be. We, as our child's role models, need both love and discipline to constructively and effectively influence our youngster.

Chapter 4

EFFECTIVE DISCIPLINE
*"Parents who are afraid to put their foot down
usually have children who step on their toes."*
(Chinese Proverb)

WALKING THE TALK

In the summer of 1999, I was invited as a guest speaker to the Hadassah National Conference in Washington, D.C. On my panel, whose theme was *Pride of the Future*, was one bright and vibrant lady who spoke about the importance of parents doing what they expect and wish their children to do. The parents, she passionately said, needed to set an example.

"It's as simple as that," she said. "If you want your children to get an education, get an education. If you want them to observe and appreciate traditions that are dear to you, observe and appreciate those traditions. It's as simple as that!"

Action speaks louder than words: *Show Them and They will Follow!* Yes, it's as simple as that, yet as complex as one can imagine. Telling alone doesn't do the trick. Providing a model which she can emulate is a far more effective approach to motivating a child to do the right thing. This is a process with checks and balances that goes on throughout a child's growing years. This is obviously not a quick fix approach. It requires self-discipline on our part. We cannot effectively set a viable example and pass on to our child something that we ourselves are not able to do. Lip service can bring only ephemeral results. It takes lots of loving patience, support, courage, and why not, appropriate humor to be or become an adequate parent.

Children have an uncanny ability to register what goes on around them, even if, at times, they seem oblivious to what's going on. Modeling provides a clear example for her to see, and therefore more compelling for her to emulate. How do we react when we receive good news? Unpleasant news? When we are verbally attacked? When we are angry? What tone of voice do we use when we reprimand our child? When we apologize? Indeed, as stressed throughout this book, what we regularly do makes a significant impression on our child -- *An acorn doesn't fall far away from its tree.* If, for instance, we repeatedly lie (even little white lies add up) to her and other people, if we break promises for no good reason, if we "yo-yo" with rules around the house and apply them only when they accommodate us, we can rest assured that our child is more likely to do the same. If we do the exact thing we tell her not to, what are the odds that she would trust our teaching when it comes to issues of drugs, alcohol, and irresponsible sex acts? Let's walk the talk! It may take time, but it sure raises the likelihood that our child would emulate appropriate and constructive behavior.

In the midst of numerous, daily family demands, we sometimes lose sight of our most important goal as our child's first teachers and role models. We become, consciously or unconsciously, inconsistent. When a child feels caught up in a double standard, the resulting effects on the child may range from mild disobedience, to disrespect, and to total defiance. When half of the time we lecture her for her inappropriate behavior such as cursing, for instance, and half of the time we don't; or we somewhat encourage her to use foul language toward third parties because they "deserve" it, we fall short of understanding that, sooner or later, she *will* use the same language with *us*. We then wonder how could something like that happen?! "I'm your mother... I'm your father, how could you say that to *me*? How could you do that to *me*?" The "Do as I say, not as I do" philosophy does not hold water with youngsters, especially those in the hormonally challenged phase of adolescence. Obviously, as pointed out earlier, we need to learn how to be ourselves self-disciplined, consistent, and have the courage to live up to our role as parents, i.e. role models.

PREREQUISITES FOR EFFECTIVE DISCIPLINE

The effectiveness of a chosen discipline approach greatly depends on each family's particularities, situations, contexts, and so on. Nonetheless, there are some particular prerequisites that parents need to learn and master in order to effectively influence their child: assertion of *parental authority*, *fairness* in our parent-child interactions, *consistency* coupled with *flexibility*, and humane and feasible family rules.

PARENTAL AUTHORITY

Parents have, by nature, the power to decide how to raise their child. They are, in many ways, the ones who shape tomorrow's society. This can be an overwhelming responsibility, to say the least. Some of us, with concern about doing this responsibility right, feel uncomfortable making final decisions, taking action, or giving orders when necessary. We constantly question ourselves if we are raising our child properly -- especially in today's "laisser-faire" parenting mentality adopted as the best parenting approach by a growing number of parents.

In nowadays' prevalent *I-do-as-I-feel-oriented* culture, many of us are uncertain and hesitant about appropriately asserting our power as the parent and the family authority figure. Consciously or unconsciously, we abdicate our legitimate parental authority and strive to be more of a "friend" than a parent to our child! There is a divine reason why we happen to be *parents* and our youngster, *a child!* And Mother Nature makes it so that being parent to our child is a *given,* becoming our child's friend is a *gift!* Like everything else in life, there is a time to be a child and a time to be a parent! There *will* be times when we doubt ourselves as parents. That is OK, or shall I say, even healthy because occasional self-doubt usually brings about self-awareness of what we do. This in turn leads to self-evaluation, which is far more constructive than being self-righteous.

Do I imply here that we must always be very serious in our role as a parent? Far from it. We can, at times, be *children* with our child, not only in order to play with her, but also as a way to empathize and better see things from her viewpoint as stated before. We all have a *child in us.* However when we know that our child needs our *experienced* loving support, we help her better when we play our role of parent. We needn't be moved only by "feelings" of the moment, or let the "child" in *us* take over and start to settle the unsettled business of our childhood through our child. We *are* the parents and the adults. Our parental authority is an essential function of childrearing. As we assert our parental authority with *fairness*, we also have to acknowledge our child's milestones, every step of the way. This can be a great motivator in her efforts to self-regulate.

FAIRNESS

Do unto others what you want others to do unto you! As pointed out earlier, parents' responsibility *vis-à-vis* house rules and regulations must be a two-way street, i.e., not expecting only our child to observe and respect these rules. We are *both*, our child AND us, expected to obey these rules. Even when a child comes to resent these rules or restrictions, she is likely to resent them less when there is a sense of fairness as they apply to everyone in the family.

This sense of fairness is more so reinforced when, from time to time, we let our child decide along with us what she thinks her penalty ought to be, given whatever offense she committed. At times, children tend to be tougher on themselves in choosing what sort of penalty they think they deserve. Parents, of course, have to tone it down -- or up if the child tries to belittle her offense.

Rules and regulations, i.e., restrictions, are much more effective when associated with benefits -- *related freedoms*. This, in and of itself, helps motivate a child to abide by a specific rule, to have the will and the patience to forego instant gratification, for instance, for a much earned freedom or privilege later on. In the long run, this association of regulations to privilege strengthens her self-discipline, the ultimate goal, which will guide her throughout the challenging years of adolescence and adulthood. Moreover, we foster a climate of trust in our parent-child relationship when we honor our end of the bargain by providing the agreed-on privilege to our child after she observed a specific rule.

Not reasonably keeping our word creates inconsistency and distrust. As we relate a certain restriction to a particular freedom, the latter must also be linked to a *related responsibility*. For example, if our youngster wants to play with her bike in a muddy backyard, because she says it is so much fun there, it must be made clear to her that she has to clean-up the bike before she can put it back in the garage. Not only does this teach her to be accountable and responsible for her actions, but also that for every freedom that we enjoy, there's also a responsibility that we have to assume.

She will eventually learn that she cannot do "whatever-I-want-to" or "I-fee-like" and expect no consequences from her actions. The sooner and earlier in life she learns this, the easier her life "out there" is likely to be. Through our consistent examples, we can teach her that *true* freedom actually comes with strings attached.

CONSISTENCY WITH APPROPRIATE FLEXIBILITY

People, and especially children, learn more effectively when they know what is expected of them and somewhat predict what possible outcomes will result from their actions -- or inaction. This, in turn, takes away a great deal of stress and anxiety from not knowing what to expect from one's actions. There is also a certain sense of security when rules and regulations are consistent.

Nonetheless, being consistent doesn't guarantee that

a child will always be on her best behavior. She *will* test, soon or later, her parents' limits; some children more so than others. This also depends on how we respond to her "tests." Do we regularly enforce our rules and regulations fairly and consistently? Do we enforce them *only* when it is convenient, and don't do so when *we* are inconvenienced? Are we sending mixed messages to the child, the clearest one being that we don't really care about her unacceptable behavior when it does not inconvenience *us*?

Being consistent AND flexible at the same time is further more effective than consistency without flexibility. *Flexibility* brings about a sense of fairness as we may come to change our position given new information and circumstances of a situation. The courage to change our position conveys the message that we are *with* her and on *her* side, we are not enforcing the rules just for the sake of doing so. Flexibility and fairness mean that when we realize that we did an injustice to our child, we must admit our error *right away* and apologize to her. We, parents, also do make mistakes, and we need to own up to them.

Both parents, for instance, don't have to agree on *all* rules of their family dynamics just for the sake of being consistent. Consistency does not need to go to such an extreme. This kind of rigidity does not really prepare a child to successfully deal with the world beyond her home. Children, in general, adapt well to reasonable, differing standards of both their parents.

My children, for instance, know the difference when I ask them to tidy up their rooms, and when their father asks them the same thing. Same thing as far as noise is concerned. Quietness for me and for my husband means two different things. Our children don't have -- or show -- any major handicap adjusting to these differing standards.

Furthermore, a child of school age needs this notion of flexibility to adapt to standards of her different teachers. Each teacher's standards often differ from those of other teachers and those from home. Bringing up a child with a flexible discipline approach thus allows her to acquire social skills that help her to appropriately dwell in the world at large. She subsequently develops common sense which, in turn, becomes her guide in how to conduct herself in different situations and contexts.

As pointed out earlier, when rules and regulations are ambiguous and inconsistent, a child is more likely going to repeatedly misbehave. The ambiguity and inconsistency fosters the law of "damned if you do, damned if you don't," and with it a certain degree of insecurity and stress. Having, preferably written, family rules in place can help a child eventually get an idea about consequences, penalties, or benefits of her actions. The likelihood of parents being inconsistent and unfair is higher when there are no explicit family rules or structure.

Sometimes, inconsistency in discipline can be brought up by *third parties*, i.e., other family members or hired caregivers who regularly interact with the child. Grandparents, for instance, have a special role and place in a child's life. Some children spend a great deal of time with, or are left in the care of, their grandparents. Some are even raised by their grandparents. Many grandparents actually look forward to being with their grandchildren. They give their grandchildren plenty of affection and a great deal of loving attention. Many are usually retired and have ample time to be with their grandchildren. This can be a real blessing as they interact and develop a relationship with their grandchildren.

People usually expect grandparents to "spoil" their grandchild. However, problems may arise when grandparents become overindulgent to a fault with their grandchild. They may start to let her behave or do things that they know full well her parents wouldn't allow, or let her get away with things that they, the grandparents, themselves didn't let their own child get away with. At this point, they have crossed the line. They are undermining our authority *vis-à-vis* our child. Clearly, it's not in the best interest of our child and ourselves that our authority is curtailed, especially when done behind our back, in a conspiratorial manner: "Don't tell mommy or daddy. This is our secret!" This is detrimental to both the child and the parent-child relationship, and even to the grandparent-grandchild relationship.

To avoid or end such a situation, parents must make it clear to their own parents, and any other caregivers, what their child is or is not allowed to do. If their wishes are not respected, by all means it's within their power to restrict their child's visits with these third parties. Yes, this can and *will* create serious frictions with concerned family members. However, our foremost responsibility as parent is first toward our child. Our parents, for instance, had their time to be parents to us. This is our time! We have the right and the power to take into our very own hands and see to it what's in our child's best interest.

Inconsistency can also come into play out of a lack of *direction* within family dynamics: parents' inadequacy or lack of motivation to learn more about parenting responsibilities. On a positive note, it's never too late to right a gone-astray situation when we realize that our inconsistency is at the root of some specific problems in our child's behavior. We can make it possible by investing time in learning the skills to be less ambiguous in our parent-child communication and have more confidence in our chosen house rules.

The first step is to objectively analyze the situation, through professional intervention if need be. Then, with appropriate coaching, address the situation. It is indeed a much greater challenge the older the child is, as both she and the parent have to learn new ways and unlearn long seated habits. As much as consistency in discipline is sought, rules and regulations must also be *humane* to raise the likelihood that she will emulate long lasting appropriate behavior.

SELF-REGULATION MAINTENANCE APPROACHES

IMPLANTING VALUES

The odds that our child will more likely be receptive to the values that matter most to us greatly depend on the way *we* live and show respect for these moral values, and the way we are enthusiastic about certain things from early on. A positive outlook on things usually motivates a child to adopt compassionate, moral values out of love for others rather than out of fear of punishment or intimidation. As she gets older and has proven mature enough, we can be confident enough to allow her to make her choices about moral values that matter the most to *her*, however difficult and disarming that may be. She is more likely to make well-informed choices when exposed to differing or even conflicting value systems provided that we have done our best to pass on these moral values from the very early years.

However, sometimes parents don't always get to care for a child from her early years. They may get an older child, i.e., over five years old or so. When this situation comes to be, the parent-child relationship is even more so challenged, because both parent and child are going from ground zero as far as early years learning and bonding are concerned. For parents and children in this situation, it means a whole different set of challenges, rules, attitudes, goals, and expectations. An older child comes with a background, package of values, ideals, and viewpoints. She has already had various learning experiences, perhaps under conditions quite different from those in her present life. As a result, the child's values, feelings, attitudes, and ideals may not be quite like her parents'.

It's a serious and tough call that parents have to make when they decide to care for an older child. If they want to shape their child so that she adopts their ideals and values, so that she shows them affection and appreciation, they may be in for a huge disappointment. However, if their wishes are to provide their child with a home and a chance to become a responsible, mature adult, then their odds as successful parents are high.

By no means is caring for or adopting an older child a questionable or bad idea. If I had to do it all over again, I'd adopt again my sister's three children, however difficult it was. This situation simply calls for different sets of expectations and a much greater effort to accept the unknown individuality of the older child. It is probably easier, if you definitely want to pass on your own ideals and moral values, that the adopted child be in her early years, from birth to around three years or so. The fact of the matter is just that adopting an older child is a much more challenging experience. But then again isn't our role of raising any child into a responsible individual challenging?

To effectively influence our youngster, we need to also learn how to talk *with*, as opposed to *to*, a child from a very young age. We have to create a home atmosphere in which we, child and parent, are motivated to explore different ideas and carry on constructive and meaningful conversations. Before long, she *will* enter the adult world. She will be in social activities in which she needs to know how to carry on conversations like a well-balanced, confident, independent, civilized, and responsible young lady. Our responsibility is to *routinely* give her the support and love she needs to get to that point, step by step, over the years. Not a small feat!

ESTABLISHING ROUTINES

In general, having a routine in terms of daily activities provides direction for family dynamics. To a growing child, an environment that is both predictable and dependable brings about less uncertainty, less stress and confusion. Healthy routines within family can be effective and helpful when they meet criteria such as flexibility, *clarity*, and consistency as explained earlier. As a child goes through different developmental changes so will routines be also appropriately modified to meet these changes -- and particular individual changes of family members. Study times, bedtimes, or chore assignments, for instance, have to be adjusted to the child's age and skill level to be meaningful.

Daily family dynamics are beneficial for both parents and the child as there tends to be less friction in deciding each and every day who is to do what and/or who did what last. There is a sense of fairness about every member chipping in their fair share into the "family basket." Both parents and child are usually less confused, disorganized, and less stressed about their obligations and duties. When routines are clear and in place, there is less nagging to get a child to do her chores, for instance. When she is not happy about her assignments, which is going to happen at one time or another, she is likely to take it out on the posted daily or weekly chore list rather than on her parents!

Flexibility also means *occasionally* making *exceptions* in the established routines, for extraordinary situations or events. Frequent exceptions perturb a sense of stability, predictability, and fairness. A child who is not the recipient of such exceptions may come to resent that her excused sibling is getting a free ride while she is carrying the extra load. Furthermore, a family routine or family rules with too many daily exceptions loses both its purpose and effectiveness since rules cannot be effective when applied according to mood, whims, or feelings of the moment.

We cannot expect a child to perform her share of household duties with enthusiasm while we, parents, constantly complain, or don't do our fair share as we ought to. Our objective and positive attitude *vis-à-vis* house rules and/or routines help her learn that, sometimes, we need to do things that are not necessarily fun, but that need to be done anyway. Routines have to be administered in a matter of fact, impersonal way, yet in a pleasant manner. We need to make it clear to our youngster that it is her responsibility, not ours, to clean her room, for instance. Usually, enforcement for an unfulfilled routine is more effective and a more meaningful learning experience when the penalty is to do the same kind of chores that should have been done in the first place except with more of the same work added.

Routines foster self-control whereby our child learns to discipline herself to do -- or not to do -- certain things. In turn, this fosters critical thinking on her part. Although they are important for all children, routines are more so important for a child who tends to be hyperactive, fearful, impulsive, or who would otherwise need constant parental supervision.

How can a family come up with its own unique yet effective family routine? During family discussions, parents and children can brainstorm and come up with a set of house rules and regulations. These rules are meant to protect both parents AND children. To make them even more "tangible," it is a good idea, although not mandatory, for parents and/or children to actually write these rules down and post them -- as a reminder between family meetings. You'd be surprised how children are uncanny at reminding us when we get out of line and don't follow the agreed upon rules!

I, for one, have been reminded on different occasions to *behave* and get back *in line*! We are all too human. We sometimes forget, get lazy, or lack the strength. This is another reason why having clear family rules is more helpful than either having none or being inconsistent with chosen ones. A sample of what house rules and regulations might be like is listed below. This may be too long or too short depending on the particulars of different families.

During family discussions, every member is encouraged to voice their opinions and to give their input. The goal here is to create a sense of shared decision-making, individual responsibility and accountability, and respect for *all* family members' opinions and feelings. There is, however, no guarantee that a family with rules and regulations in place won't have any problems. All families have to face problems at one time or another. That's a given. However, a family with a structure and a mechanism *in place*, i.e., rules and regulations, is better prepared to address problems and/or conflict situations much more effectively. The bottom line is that, even in disagreements, members of a family with a somewhat clear structure and direction interact as a support unit instead of a group of individuals who happen to live under one roof.

HOUSE RULES

HONESTY: 1. If any one of these house rules doesn't make any sense or is irrelevant, let's discuss it, and see if it needs to be modified.
2. All questions are welcome and encouraged. There is no such a thing as a stupid question.

RESPECT: 1. Use of swear words or foul language to express frustration or anger is not acceptable. Describe how you feel and how you'd like whomever you have problem(s) with to address the situation. No name calling, but describe how you feel.
2. Egoism doesn't belong in our family vocabulary. However, before you use anything that belongs to somebody else, please first ask permission from that person.

ORDER: 1. When you move something, please put it back where you took it after use.
2. If you don't know how to use something, please ask first someone else who knows how to use it to show you how.

DAILY SCHEDULE: 1. Breakfast must consist of healthy food (cereals, fruits, etc.), and a big no to sweets, cakes cookies, and the like.
2. During weekdays, bedtime is **8:30 PM**, except if you have to finish homework. At **9:45 PM** at the latest, everyone is in bed and lights are turned off.

HYGIENE: Everyone must <u>strictly</u> use their own toothbrush, comb, towel, and cup. These items mustn't, under any circumstances, be shared.

ENVIRONMENT : To save energy, always turn off lights when not in the room, turn off tap after use, turn off radio when not listening to it. Please put in the recycling boxes all that can be recycled.

SECURITY: <u>Never open the door</u> to anyone you don't know, or you know but feel uncomfortable ...
<u>Never get into a car</u> with anyone you don't know; or you know but have a funny feeling about and without prior permission from us.

No one can tell how much or how well a child between the age of two and four understands or learns from regular family discussions. Nevertheless, including everybody in the family discussions forms participatory habits for the child from very early on. When a child gets used to the dynamics of family discussions, the process will not be alien to her when she needs help or voices her concerns.

For various reasons however, some families prefer not to implement any agreed upon routines. They somehow don't find it beneficial to have a given structure for their family dynamics. And there may well be a good point to this position. Too rigid a family dynamic structure may lead to stressed out children. Obviously, there must be moderation to everything. Having *reasonable* -- as opposed to overscheduled -- routines is an effective approach to foster self-regulation in children. Furthermore, we can reinforce self-regulation through routines that have systems for recognizing and acknowledging children's efforts in adopting acceptable behavior.

ACKNOWLEDGING PROGRESS

We help our child sustain her enthusiasm in emulating appropriate behavior by showing her our appreciation for her efforts and progress. We need to learn not to take for granted the little "miracles" that she does.

Children usually like to do things like "big boys" or "big girls." They want to do right. It is an instinctive drive to want to feel bigger and more powerful. Our reassurance is a great feedback to how she is doing. It is an affirmation that we really are paying attention to her, and that we, indeed, care about her. *She* matters a whole world to us!

When a child thinks she has done a good job, she is usually proud to show it off to her parents.

"See how I can tie my shoes all by myself," says three-year-old Pete to his father Bradley.

"See how I can clean my room so good," says nine-year-old Simone to her mother Meg.

"Mommy do you remember when I couldn't reach the table, and you had to put books on my chair," says five year old Kevin to Leah, his mother. "Look at me now, I'm so big, I can reach it," he says, looking up at his mother with a big grin on his face.

"Yes, Kev, you are such a big boy now, and you can do so many things... oh my!" "I'm so very proud of you," Leah says looking at him and tenderly roughing her son's hair.

"And one day, Sammy will also be sooo big enough and he can even reach the table like me, mommy," Kevin says, looking at his little brother sitting in his high chair.

"Daddy, do you remember when I didn't know how to read," says eight-year-old Deborah to her father. "Now I can finish a whole book in just *one* day!"

"Oh yes! I am so proud of you! And I like it very much when you tell me the stories that you read," replies Deborah's father.

Obviously, five-year-old Kevin and eight-year-old Deborah want their parents to validate what they think they are capable of doing. They, indeed, want to show how they use their "magic within."

To acknowledge a child's progress appropriately, again, we need to see our child's efforts from her viewpoint. We have to acknowledge her progress even if the task isn't done the way we would like to be done. Our support and feedback can but reinforce her sense of self-confidence and independence in her judgment, which in turn leads to self-worth and self-esteem.

The *unconditional* acceptance provides her with the strong foundation she needs for her self-esteem even when we either agree or disagree with her ideas. It is also this foundation that provides her with the self-confidence she needs to resist *negative* peer pressure concerning issues of drugs, sex, or alcohol during her adolescence years. She will eventually be much more inclined to emulate positive peer pressure such as postponing having sex, or resisting trying to become "popular" through destructive behavior. As much as giving her our feedback for her efforts can encourage and sustain her efforts, so do our *praise* and *encouragement*.

PRAISE AND ENCOURAGEMENT

According to the *Webster Collegiate Dictionary*, *praise* means expressing appreciation for accomplishment of some sort. We praise our child when she emulates responsible behavior, especially when she takes the initiative on her own. Praise can be either *verbal* or *non-verbal*.

Verbal praise includes sentences such as, "Good job! Excellent work! You did great, Caroline!"

Non-verbal praise includes things such as a pat on the child's back, a hug, a smile, putting a youngster's drawings on the wall, or displaying her trophies in the house.

There is a caveat. Praise is more meaningful when conveyed for *concrete* deeds, achievements, and accomplishments that the child did or is doing. Unsubstantiated praise eventually leads to empty self-esteem and *inflated ego*, i.e., masked low self-esteem. A child used to getting unsubstantiated praise may start to expect praise even when she misbehaves! As much as praise is effective when related to concrete deeds, it is much more meaningful when it is descriptive and *specific* rather than *general*.

"I see, you put your toys back in the toy box, Tricia! Excellent job!" Kathy says to her daughter as the latter is putting her toys back into the box while humming the "Clean up" song from the *Barney Show*. Kathy's praise to her daughter is much more effective and encouraging rather than if she'd merely said, "Good girl, Tricia," to her daughter.

Even though both situations are meant to encourage the child, Kathy's first remarks are more *specific* than the second ones. General praise tends to be rather evaluative of Tricia's *total* person, which is, in many ways, erroneous. The conscious or unconscious evaluation of a child's total character is unrealistic and can be detrimental. What happens when Tricia does something unacceptable? Do we tell her, "Bad girl?" Do we reject and negate everything that Tricia *is*? We cannot throw out the child with the bath water!

When we make total personality evaluative remarks to a child, there usually is a tendency to exaggerate things. These exaggerations transform the well-meant praise into hollow statements, distorting the entire purpose of praise: encouragement to emulate acceptable behavior. Obviously, it takes some learning, tact, and courage to praise well. Praise is a way we *reward* our child for her accomplishments and efforts.

REWARDING

A reward is a material or immaterial prize *earned* for responsible behavior. It is a form of recompense and encouragement. The more we know about our child's special and individual interests, likes and dislikes, the better we are in finding effective rewards that are likely to motivate her.

We have, however, to differentiate a *reward* and a *bribe*. A reward is something *earned* by a child for responsible deed or behavior, while a *bribe* is a payoff to "buy off" a child into complying with a rule, or into doing something. A reward fosters genuine enthusiasm, i.e., inner strength in adopting acceptable behavior. It is usually long lasting, while a bribe brings an immediate, expected result, *albeit* short lived. Bribes usually promote a what's-in-it-for-me attitude in the child.

Rewards can be either *material* or *immaterial*. Material rewards can be in the form of buying a special thing or toy for our child, or giving her extra money to add to her allowance, etc. Immaterial reward can be something like letting the child watch T.V. for an extra length of time, or letting her use the family car more often, etc.

Although rewarding children with material things hasn't been one of my favorite motivators to foster acceptable behavior, this approach proves to be effective for other families given their special situations and contexts. Giving material rewards, i.e., money, for extraordinary chores, such as when a child cleans her parents' car, for instance, can prove to be a great motivator. The danger of using only material rewards is that, often, it leads a child to view material things as symbols of approval -- and even of love. Once there is an association between love and material things in the child's mind, parents have to continually supply her with material things to influence her into doing anything. As stated before, there is almost no genuine enthusiasm to do or emulate appropriate behavior just for the sake of doing good or doing the right thing.

Sooner or later, families with more than one child may come to realize that where one type of reward or even parenting approach works well with one child, the same approach doesn't quite bring the same result with their other child. Even for families with a single child, a parenting approach that works well at a certain time may become obsolete when the environment, age, context, situation, or state of child's body and mind have changed. We therefore need to make adjustments and re-adjustments to modify and *tailor* our parenting approach to effectively respond to each individual child's particular situations.

TAILORING DISCIPLINE APPROACH

From infancy through adolescence, each child experiences developmental phases differently. Even though it would be easier to uniformly apply family rules and regulations to all children, some modifications are often necessary given that every child is unique.

Mira and Chuck's sons, Alan and Joel, were quite different from the very moment they were born. Alan was quiet, calm, and slept most of the time. Joel was completely the opposite. He was very alert, awake, and cried most of the time. Even when they moved into their terrific twos, Alan rarely had dramatic temper tantrums while his brother Joel was a full blown case of a dramatic tantrum thrower. It took Joel longer than his brother to calm down. Mira and Chuck found themselves learning different approaches to be able to meet their son Joel's needs. Although their parenting style was uniform regarding both children, there were significant variations in how they approached each *indi-*

vidual child during challenging situations.

Tailoring parenting approaches to each child's individual characteristics more likely enables every family member to excel at their unique competence. In such an atmosphere, parents and children learn how to take care of themselves, value their uniqueness, and celebrate their individual accomplishments.

As said before, even with the best intentions in the world for the child, we parents wind up making mistakes. We may feel, at one time or another, as if we fail our child, and thereby get ridden with guilt. This may get to a degree where some of us become handicapped from doing our parenting responsibility as best as we could. What do we do when this happen?

FEELINGS OF GUILT

Many parents (including me) have felt, at one time or another, some guilt about the way they are raising their children. Guilt is a feeling of self-reproach for committed or imagined offenses. It also can come from a sense of inadequacy that we may feel at some points during our parenting journey. This feeling of guilt is not, however, always a negative thing as pointed out earlier. If it is *merited* and *justified*, guilt can be a *positive catalyst* for behavior change. It can motivate parents to step back, think, and question their stand on an issue or situation. *Ipso facto*, parents would eventually seek appropriate course of action to be able to remedy the situation. When parents behave in ways that are inconsiderate, destructive, or obnoxious *vis-à-vis* their child, for instance, a justifiable and *healthy* sense of guilt can cause them to think about their behavior and the impact it has on their child. As they evaluate their behavior, they are likely to be motivated to remedy them.

When a child shows feelings of guilt AND it is merited, we are not helping her if and when we try, by all means, to prevent her from having those feelings, because *we* believe that her *self-esteem* would crumble or her feelings toward *us* are in jeopardy. When she *appropriately* shows feelings of guilt, it is a sign that she has internalized moral values about right and wrong. Having made that part of her personality, she is more likely bound to get a *healthy* sense of guilt and discomfort when she does something she knows is unacceptable. We don't need to readily jump to "It's OK, it's all right!" when our youngster gets sad after she has done something unacceptable. In all actuality, her *appropriate* feeling of guilt conveys a sense of *self-analysis* resulting from the moral values she has internalized. Consequently, she minds what she does and says.

Children also need to be taught that their behaviors have an effect on other people, *even* on adults. Their behavior can cause pain, discomfort, and/or sadness. If parents jump to "It's OK," and quickly dismiss her misbehavior when she shows remorse, we are thereby giving her the impression that we don't really mind how she behaves. Consequently, she may not have a clear sense of direction about our values and standards for behavior. In all likelihood, she may wind up thinking that we really don't care about what she does or about her!

It is, however, completely out of line and cruel, to say the least, for parents to try to control their child by unfairly playing on her emotions. This is called *manipulation* -- and psychological abuse to some extent. Even though this tactic may work in getting a child into complying with our wishes and desires, we parents are, nevertheless, teaching our youngster an unhealthy way to get cooperation. Children can learn this pretty fast! And we are to regret it. It's an unfair, heavy load on a child's shoulders to think that *she* is responsible for her parents' anger, sadness, and/or unhappiness! It is both immature of us and destructive for the child. In such situation, she is most likely to think that *she,* not *her actions,* is the cause of her parents' personal problems such as divorce, sickness, or even death.

As pointed out earlier, as much as we want to let our child know when her inappropriate behavior causes pain, we also must greatly stress the pride, joy, happiness, and fun that *she* brings into our lives through her efforts, achievements, cooperation, and, above all, just for being her own person, i.e., who she is. In so doing, we are better prepared to face problems when (not if) they come up into our parent-child relationship.

SUMMARY

It is a very fine line, accepting our parental authority and knowing how to use it appropriately and effectively. Obviously, both the child and her parents need self-discipline to develop a sound, well-balanced parent-child relationship. Parental authority, fairness, humane and flexible family rules and regulations are capital to giving direction and structure to a chosen discipline approach. The structure provides both parent and child with a system of checks and balances for their interactions and enables parents to effectively address behavior problems when they arise.

BEHAVIOR CRISIS MANAGEMENT

"No man commands ably unless he has himself obeyed discipline."
(Latin Proverb)

Our responsibility as parents is, *first*, to teach our child the skills he needs to constructively dwell in different situations. We coach him as to how he can emulate constructive behavior. Coaching a child sounds simple, yet it is a very complex task. We need to give him structure and direction, as stated earlier, through rules and regulations, and most convincingly through our own behavior.

Second, we need to consistently and appropriately enforce these rules and regulations to see to it that our child learns that there is a relationship between his actions and subsequent consequences, that there are rules and limitations to be respected in a civilized society. There is only one guarantee for us: there *will* be problems when raising a child. Our child *will* misbehave at one time or another despite our best efforts to set an example for him. What do we do then when this comes to be?

I'll start by giving children credit; children often have good intentions when they do certain things and behave in certain ways. Given their limited knowledge and experience in life, they are more likely inclined to choosing behavior for which they cannot quite foresee the consequences. From their misjudgments, accidents follow, and they get in trouble.

When a child misbehaves, and doesn't know what to do, or behaves as if he knew what to do and continues to blow it, we have to step in and provide him with appropriate structure and direction. Even though it is difficult to look beyond a child's misdeed, our focus must nonetheless be on finding lessons to be learnt from the mistake(s). We have to learn some parenting skills that will enable us to be in a better position to provide constructive criticism to our child. *Temporary distancing* and *change of the child's environment* are but two of the various techniques that can be quite effective. One of the least effective approaches is either for parents to repress their frustrations or "blow up" into serious rage when their child misbehaves despite parents' best efforts. How do temporary distancing and change of environment work?

DISTANCING

Even when parents know from experience that every crisis has its own end, they often feel overwhelmed in the heat of the moment. When their patience runs out, both the youngster and the parent(s) are better off taking some time off from each other. Parents need to distance themselves to be able to calmly reflect on their child-rearing responsibility and let their emotions of the moment get some time to cool off. Eventually, they will feel refreshed, physically and emotionally, and become ready to see the situation much more clearly, and thus address their child's misbehavior much more constructively.

Distancing can be either *formal*, such as a child going on school trips or going to summer camp; or *informal,* such as the child going on play dates or family visits. Distancing can also be *long* or *short term.* Getting someone to baby-sit, or taking a child to a relative for a short visit while you go out, or having him sleepover at his friend's are some examples of *short-term informal* distancing.

Short-term distancing is usually much more effective and works best when the child is in his early years, i.e.., before adolescence. Sending a child for an entire summer vacation to visit with relatives, for instance, is an example of a long-term informal distancing.

A *long-term formal* distancing example would be sending a child to a sleep-away camp for an entire summer, or sending him to live in a boarding school during a school year.

Sometimes it takes only a few minutes away from the misbehaving child for him to catch his breath and for us to be able to collect ourselves. This is especially so with our terrific twos. In this case, *time-out*, another form of short-term distancing, may work wonders.

Time Out

Time out is a period during which a child is sent to a particular place where he is temporarily not allowed to engage in any activities. Time-out works differently for each individual child.

One afternoon, Stacey's three-year-old daughter Dana asked for an ice-cream cone. She asked her mother for another right after the first one. She hadn't

even finished those two when she wanted another...
right away! When her mother said "no," Dana started
whining and throwing a tantrum.

"I want another ice-cream, NOW!" Dana said while
screaming and stomping her feet on the ground.

This is how Stacey learned to address her daughter's tantrums by using the time-out technique.

First, she acknowledged her daughter's feelings of
frustration for not getting what she wanted right away.

"I know you must be really upset not getting another ice-cream cone. Mommy cannot give you any
more. You've already had two. That makes you really
upset!"

"Yeah," screamed Dana, "I want another NOW!"
she said as she threw on the floor what was left of the
second ice-cream cone she was holding while a piece of
the first was on the table.   "It's OK if you feel like
crying," Stacey said to her daughter. At this point
Dana, with ice-cream smeared all over her hands and
face, was already sniffling, crying and making a scene.

Second, as Dana was carrying on, Stacey took her
to a corner of the dinning room, and put Dana on a
small stool.

"You sit here, Dana, until you calm down. You
know what? You can think of your calming 'inside-
magic' too!" Stacey said while putting down her daughter in a matter of fact way.

"How long do you think you'll make your calming
inside-magic work? Two or three minutes?" Stacey
asked her daughter while showing her two and then
three fingers.

"Mmmm.." Dana usually doesn't talk, but would
only show up her three fingers while she purses her lips
up.

Almost always children choose the longest alternative, three minutes in Dana's situation above. And almost always they stop whining or crying after only a minute or two, before their time is up -- provided that the child doesn't get *any* kind of attention.

"You know you still have one minute left," Stacey told her daughter when Dana stopped crying and looked as if she had enough of it.

"Mmm..." Dana said shaking her head sideways, meaning "no." "I wanna stop now... I don't wanna cry anymore!" Dana told her mother as she wiped off tears from her face -- smearing her face more so with chocolate-strawberry mush.

For this time-out "whining buster" technique to work effectively, once we explain to our child that the time for her whining and/or crying starts (and she is in a safe place), it's time to hang in there, parents. Just as Stacey did in the example above. The crucial determinant here is not to pay *any* attention whatsoever to the child's carrying on. Otherwise, she still gets the attention, however negative it may be, from you. To some children, *any* attention, even negative attention, is better than none.

It is very difficult to go on whining or complaining when no one pays attention. Whining and tantrums are, after all, better performed when there is an audience! It takes a lot of patience and courage to constructively *ignore* a misbehaving child.

IGNORING AND REDIRECTING

Ignoring is a parenting approach that uses a non intervention technique when a child exhibits inappropriate and/or annoying behavior in the hope that, by not making it a big deal, the child would eventually be demotivated in engaging in the unwanted behavior. This is another form of distancing, *albeit* emotionally. Ignoring can take a while to bring about the desired result. As mentioned earlier, it's not easy to ignore a child's behavior that we dislike. It requires willpower, lots of patience, and perseverance. Behavior such as temper tantrums, whining, or any other annoying acts -- typical of a child being a child -- can be modified by ignoring.

When a small child repeatedly does annoying things that are typical of a child trying to "attract" his parents' attention, ignoring is an appropriate, if not the best, approach. This must be done both in *actions* and *words*. It means giving absolutely no attention. Not looking at the child, i.e., not showing either exasperation or annoyance. Parents behave as if nothing were happening. This is not easy.

Sometime *redirecting* a child's energy to another activity rather than ignoring can be very effective in stopping a misbehavior. Asking, for instance, a question that re-channels a child's attention to another acceptable activity can be a starting point. A caveat here, as it is for any other approach, is to not overdo it. The same goes for distracting a child from carrying on with an unacceptable behavior. We may at times use different ways to distract our child from keeping up with an unwanted behavior by giving him a toy, money, or using television or gaming devices as both a distraction and a distancing device.

TELEVISION AND ELECTRONIC GAMING DEVICES

Television and other gaming devices are frequently

used as baby-sitters. We let our child watch anything and everything for as long as he wants so long as he either doesn't get upset because we tell him no and we don't want him to pester us, or for any other number of reasons. Children, especially younger ones, are like sponges. They suck in and absorb all that goes on in their environment. Television is a medium that can and does expose youngsters to a great deal of the good *as well as* the ills in our society. The negatives often seem to be much more fascinating than the good -- evil inclination in human nature to be attracted to the "forbidden fruit?!" When more than three or four hours a day are spent in front of a TV set or electronic gaming devices without any supervision, a child is more likely to start emulating and acting out much of what he sees on TV or in these video games.

There are some extreme cases of unsupervised TV viewing that lead to fatal casualties. In a Florida court case in July of 1999, a twelve-year-old boy killed a six-year-old girl left in the care of his mother. The mother had used TV for years as a baby-sitter for her son. She let him watch anything he wanted for as long as he felt like it. This is but one of the many extreme cases of a negative impact of unsupervised television viewing by children -- especially those in the early years – that are, unfortunately, often reported in the news.

There is a great deal of evidence that it's in our child's best interest that we supervise and monitor her TV viewing in order to minimize exposure to programs that glamorize violence, sex, drug abuse, or bullying. Without a doubt, the media has its fair share of responsibility for the ills and problems in our society today. However, we cannot go on blaming the media when we don't do our own fair share of being our child's first teachers. Most habits are formed very early on. We are responsible for what goes on in *our* homes. What we bring and don't bring in our homes is up to *us*.

When a child is in his early years, from birth to about eight or so years of age, we are able to control many facets of his life. We greatly determine what, how, where, and with whom he spends his time. We pretty much determine what he eats, wears, and with which friends he plays. This *is* also the time when we can teach him good habits about watching TV. We can determine what programs, shows, and movies our child is allowed to watch, and for how long. After all, there are also some good TV programs and shows for children. Being a child that he is, our child will not good-heartedly accept TV viewing rules without any resistance. We have, nonetheless, to stick to it. In the long run, it will eventually become *normal* to him to know and accept that he cannot watch TV every day or all day long, or any programs or shows.

If our child exhibits inappropriate behavior when he is in a certain environment despite our efforts to influence otherwise, *changing that environment* would more likely be an approach to consider.

CHANGING THE ENVIRONMENT

Three ways to change an environment would be to subtract the child from the environment, to rearrange it, or add to it. Parents frequently *rearrange, add to, or subtract from* our home things that may jeopardize the safety of a child. We *childproof* the house even before our child starts to move around. As said earlier, this is a preventive step to avoid accidents that can even be fatal when our child starts moving around the house. At the same time, we also add appropriate toys and things that foster his curiosity without risking his safety.

A very simple example of subtracting from the environment is *not* leaving, for instance, cookies accessible to a two, three, or four years old child. Only telling him not to eat any cookies until after dinner will not be sufficient. This can only work when the child is really full and not tempted by the sight of the cookies. And even so, we know that a child in that age range is usually fond of cookies and hasn't grasped yet his impulses, especially those having to do with hunger. The best alternative would be to put the cookies out of his reach, if not out of his sight.

I remember learning this the hard way when my son Alex graduated from nursery school. He was four. I decided to make him a huge dinosaur shaped carrot cake for his graduation. After I baked it, I put it on a small table in the kitchen to cool it down before I decorated it. When we came back from his graduation ceremony, the entire apartment was smelling the cake. I explained to my son that after his Daddy came back from work, we'd celebrate his graduation, and he'd cut the cake. He said yes he would wait until after his Daddy got home. The next thing I knew, my little guy was going back and forth, back and forth, from the kitchen to where he was playing with his baby sister. As he came near me, I could see a brownish ring around his mouth, and he smelled of cake. I went to the kitchen, and sure enough, part of the dinosaur's belly was gone! The sight was hilarious! I was ready to burst out laughing, but I collected myself, and put on a serious face in order to make my point that he was not supposed to eat the cake, as we had agreed earlier, and that he had to ask first any way. Deep down, I knew that it was mostly my own judgment, or rather misjudgment, of the situation that was at fault.

When a child constantly misbehaves when he is in company of certain relatives, friends, or peers, and usually doesn't behave so when he is away from such company, the ideal approach would be to restrict such visits, i.e., subtract the child from such unwanted influence.

When Emily's son, Anthony, was around three and was in a three-day nursery school, he played a great deal with one of his friends, Spruce. Emily realized that every time her son played with Spruce at Spruce's house, Anthony became a little too physical and started using swear words and words like "stupid, "dumb," and "moron." When Emily asked him what those words meant, Anthony didn't have a clue. Emily decided to have a talk with Amber, Spruce's mother, a very down-to-earth, single parent. Amber explained to Emily that she didn't like it either when Spruce exhibited this behavior. Unfortunately, Spruce had to spend a great deal of time with his two cousins, in their early teens, who were baby-sitting him. Amber had a full time job. Spruce and his cousins watched lots of violent TV shows with lots of foul language. Emily decided then to have Spruce over to her house so that he could play with Anthony. She never again let her son go to Spruce's house.

Most importantly, we have to pay attention to the *real cause* of our child's misbehavior. If we simply address the symptoms such as whining, crying, bad mouthing, or bullying, all the remedies we may come up with would only be temporary quick fixes. *Understanding* the reasons why a child misbehaves is the first step to helping modify his behavior with long lasting results.

UNDERSTANDING WHY A CHILD MISBEHAVES

A child misbehaves for various reasons ranging from attention, power struggle, expectations, separation anxiety, health conditions, to sibling rivalry. These are but a few of the potential reasons at the root of a child's inappropriate behavior. The most prevalent reason is unequivocally communication or rather *mis*communication within parent-child interactions.

We may often *assume* that a child understands what *we* expect of him. Oftentimes what the child believes his parents expect of him may be quite a different thing than what parents believe him to understand. He undoubtedly winds up doing what *he* thinks are his parents' expectations.

As stated previously, it comes down to the basics of an effective, *two-way* communication between parent and child. *We* need to learn how to make sure that our child understands what we expect of him, and what he expects of us.

EXPECTATIONS

Mismatch in expectations often gets in the way of a healthy parent-child communication. Are our expectations of our child reasonable? How does a typical child behave? How do children generally behave?

Children are naturally noisy, active, self-centered, demanding, impulsive, and usually unpredictable. Those are the *given!* They come along with the "package," so to speak. Expecting otherwise is a problem in and of itself. Children challenge our expectations of calm, order, and tranquility. Even though some of their behaviors are unpleasant, they must nonetheless be *tolerated.*

Accepting these harmless yet annoying children's behaviors is accepting children for what they ought to be: children, and not *little adults*. Accepting and tolerating some of these behaviors with good grace doesn't, however, mean that we approve of and expect these behaviors to continue without appropriate intervention. It's not a green light for our child to do whatever he pleases without any consideration for other people's well-being. This is when rules and regulations within a family come in handy as they provide structure and direction as to how a child learns about enjoying his own rights and respecting those of other people.

We will feel challenged, especially with our adolescent child who is more likely to get angry at us. His anger toward us can be disarming. We may feel rejected, and, consequently, we tend to take it personally. "How dare you, after all we've done for you? How dare you challenge *me*. i.e., reject *me*?" But if and when we get beyond this numbing feeling of rejection, when we can de-personalize his anger and *even* expect it at different moments of his life, we can then be in a better position to provide him with effective and constructive guidance regardless.

Sometimes we expect too much from a growing youngster who is trying hard to get his act together. Does this mean that we should expect less and settle for the "normal teenage ways?" For his sake, I don't think so. We still have to expect from him reasonable, acceptable behavior as we need to be reasonable role models for him. What's "normal" for some children may not be normal for others. There must be a balance between a child's abilities and expectations. Let's give him credit that he will have the best intentions to do right, and that he *will* do all right -- provided that we have in place an open *communication system* in our parent-child interactions.

COMMUNICATION SYSTEM

Communication, defined as a channel to exchange ideas and opinions between two or more people, is the most powerful tool for parents to stay in touch with what is going on in their child's life. Open communication within the parent-child relationship is an effective control tool for fairness, healthy discipline, and constructive criticism. It makes it possible for family members to stay connected and have meaningful interactions. To be effective, a communication system requires ongoing control mechanisms such as daily conversations, weekly activities, and regular *family conferences* during which family members discuss their concerns, family rules and regulations, procedures for conflict resolution, family responsibilities, and fun and educational activities. Children learn slowly and tend to forget quickly. We, therefore, have to constantly reaffirm these rules and regulations through regular family conferences.

FAMILY CONFERENCES

In general, people usually decide to have a conference when there is a problem rather than when there is none. Having a system in place with regular family discussions may prove helpful in preventing some problems from happening or from getting out of hand. The frequency of these family conferences may be set for once a month, or once every two or three months depending on the need of family members. A family conference is an open forum for discussion during which children are empowered to voice their opinions and concerns about anything, including family *rules* and regulations.

There are two broad kinds of rules: short and long term. A *short term* rule is a command given spontaneously to a child about a particular task to be done *immediately*, a conduct to be modified according to a particular situation or context. It is rather mechanical.

"Please, don't pick up those flowers, Mia!"

"Please, eat your vegetables, Vince!"

"Kate, please go to the playground!"

These are but a few of the short term commands engendering immediate results.

A *long term* rule is a command that must be enforced over and over again; it is habit forming rather than mechanical.

"Mona, please wash your hands before you eat!"

"Todd, please take your plate from the table after you eat!"

"Please do your homework before you go play with your dog, Andrew!"

Do regular family meetings prevent family rules from being broken, or a family from having any problems at all? As stated before, problems are inevitable even for a healthy family. My husband and I went through a crash course learning about how to raise three older children, in their teen and preteen years, when we had been raising two small children under five years of age. The parent-child *honeymoon time*, a time during which a child is less critical of his parents, was coming to an end for the three of them, coupled with the fact that they were just entering their adolescent years, and they had just lost their mother, and then their father in a very short period of two years!

Our biggest concern was to continue what their parents couldn't as best as we could while, at the same time, develop a trusting, supportive relationship with the two younger ones. Needless to say, we made mistakes along the way despite our best intentions. Having children in two distinct age groups, and adjusting our parenting approaches became a very challenging responsibility. Even though we had to modify some of our *house rules*, I was neither able nor willing to change *everything* to fit the upbringing of the new set of children. We wanted to pass on our values, some of which were quite different from those of our older children. This fact, no doubt, also created challenges for them as well. A couple of big issues stood out.

First, our three older children were of a different faith. Out of respect for my deceased sister's (the children's mother) religious convictions, my husband and I wanted them to continue to practice the faith in which my sister and her husband had raised them -- and would have wanted their children to follow. We saw to it that the boys, who were not confirmed, were confirmed, and saw to it that they attended church services regularly. As some parents of adolescents may have already realized, regardless of faith, adolescents need a little more than suggestions to regularly attend services. In the beginning we went with them to their house of worship for special occasions such as their parents' birth and death anniversaries, first communion, and confirmation. Every time we explained to both sets of children, and much more so to the two younger ones, why we were going to the older children's house of worship, why each set of children needed to observe their religious holidays, and why everyone should be proud of their own faith and respectful of the others'.

Second, we made it clear (mostly to our older children) that in their new family there were not chores for only girls or only boys. Everybody, regardless of gender, had to chip into the "family basket." Once, years before, when I visited my sister's family, one of my nephews had repeatedly made reference to some chores as being "girls' duties, not for boys," and *vice versa*. I wanted to make it clear from the start that there were no division of chores by gender in their new home. Luckily, this didn't create any significant problems; we created together a daily chore chart to end the unending discussion of who should do what and when.

The third challenge was about communication and interaction between old and young children. As much as I wanted the two youngest children to be polite to and considerate of the older ones, I also needed to explain to the older children that they *also* had to do the same towards the younger ones. The older ones had some adjustments to make in this regard, not only *vis-à-vis* the two little ones, but also and especially among themselves. They had to express their frustrations and sibling rivalries not by shaming one another (the sister had a tendency to tease one of her young brothers about wetting his bed) or calling each other names. Above all, getting physical (the boys were very physical with each other when they came) was in the don't-even-think-about-it zone; it had to stop immediately. And it did. We helped them learn how to express their frustrations and anger through constructive discussion.

What helped the most in addressing all the above three main issues were the family meeting discussions that we were having, once a week, when the three older children joined our family. As we all were getting used to the new set of house rules, and the older children started to feel at home, we started having our family meeting discussions every two weeks and then once a month later on. As the years went by, we came to settle for one meeting every other month thereafter and whenever one was needed. During these meetings we encouraged them to *actively* bring their opinions and inputs. To the new set of children, even though family meetings were not new for them, discussing everything openly and matter-of-factly, even conflicting opinions, was a *quasi* new thing.

Slowly, our new set of children started to voice their opinions, concerns, and suggestions. We will never know how much participation they would have had if they had either known us well since their early years, or if they had had a similar family discussion style before. However challenging it was to abruptly adjust to a new set of children, we did the best we could to learn how we could help them adjust to the adolescent changes they were going through. Our regular conferences somewhat enabled us to have structure and direction on how to face these problems as a family.

As some of us may have realized, family conferences are not always effective. The reasons may be due to various elements such as time allocated to the discussion, and openness and objectivity about issues at hand. One of the most important factors to take into consideration on how effective a conference turns out is also a child's disposition and his *state of mind.*

CHILD'S STATE OF MIND

A child's physical and emotional state play an important role in how he behaves; our expectations of him must also adapt appropriately. The more reasonable, realistic, and feasible our expectations and demands are, the higher the likelihood that he will be more cooperative and less resistant to these expectations and demands. When our expectations or rules create a *win-win* situation, and benefit both parents and the child, the latter is more likely to abide by these rules.

To create a win-win parent-child relationship, we have to listen to and also understand what the child expects of us as mentioned earlier. He will eventually learn that his needs and/or wants indeed *matter* to us. In so doing, we create a sense of *reciprocity* in this relationship. There will be exceptional situations when we have to bend a rule and let our youngster not observe it in a specific context. When he is sick, for example, he doesn't obviously have to do his daily chores of setting up the table for dinner. Clearly, he is not making up any excuses *not* to do his chores. However, when we know that our youngster is looking for excuses and doesn't take on his responsibilities, we simply need to let him know that his objections and/or excuses are not accepted. Period. Put your foot down, Mom or Dad.

A child's misbehavior may also come to be because of intense emotions such as *fear*. When, for instance, a child wakes up in the middle of the night screaming or running into his parents' bedroom because there are monsters in his room, what he needs at that very moment is sympathy and comfort, not criticism, advice, or lecture of any kind. All he needs is reassurance that he will be OK. This is not the time to try to convince him that the monsters he saw are not real. There will be time for discussion about his fear later on. However, if he wants to talk about it right away, by all means, let's encourage him to do so. Not giving him appropriate attention or discouraging him to talk will more likely intensify his fear. When significant changes are happening in the family such as a move, birth of a sibling, death of a loved one, or divorce, nightmares are not unusual.

As pointed out earlier, parents who have more than one child may realize that each one of their children needs different degrees of attention. This is, obviously, because children have different personalities, situations, and circumstances. Some of us, consciously or unconsciously, may begin to pay *lesser* attention to children who demand less attention in favor of the more demanding ones. This can, and often does lead to a serious problem, when and if the situation is not addressed. Actually, if and when we really listen to what children say and *don't say*, they have their own way of making it clear that they are being left out. This is even before the situation becomes a real problem.

When a child continues to be ignored, for instance, he is more likely to either start building up resentment and act out toward his parents or get hostile toward the sibling who is getting all the attention. He may start whining, crying, or being rude and uncooperative. Children's typical mis-behaviors are hereunder grouped into two broad categories: those related to the early years and those related to teenagers.

EARLY YEARS: BIRTH - PRE-TEEN

While some child experts are for the theory that states children are born *"tabla rasa,"* i.e., unwritten, blank slate, others go for the one that says children are born with some pre-*disposed* attitudes. Regardless of which theory child experts support, many of them agree that children's behavior at birth is mainly driven by their *instinctive* impulses. When they are hungry, hurt, uncomfortable, they fuss and cry. When they are happy, they make cooing, happy sounds.

Through their interactions with the child, consciously or unconsciously, parents start to educate, instill, and shape their little one. As the child grows older, he starts to interact with the world around him. When he is around two years old or so, he comes to realize that his parents cannot always anticipate all his needs or wants; he is a separate person from his parents. He goes into his first *identity crisis*. He expresses his frustrations mostly through fits and tantrums.

Tantrums And Other Misbehavior

At certain developmental stages much more than others, a child usually defies his parents as he tries to establish his own person. This starts with the two-year-olds, also referred to as the terrible-twos, terrific-twos, or tumbling-twos. For the terrific two, *"no"* is one of his favorite words, if not *the* favorite word.

I once thought that toddlers within this age range overuse the word "no" because they hear a lot of "no, nos," from their parents who don't want to let their child get into unsafe places where his curiosity takes him. I decided that I would use a longer word instead, a word that would also mean "no." I started using the word *"negatif,"* French for "negative" instead of "no." I'd shake my index finger from side to side in a "no" sign. Well, was I outsmarted! Both my younger children, son and daughter, used the word "no!"

At such a critical age, to be separate from his parents also means doing the *contrary* of whatever parents want him to do. Much of the time, the child will do the contrary just for the sake of contradicting his parents. Also, our "terrific two" cannot quite express his intense emotions because of his limited vocabulary and maturity. Every parent who has had a full-blown tantrum case with a "terrible two" knows how trying this can be. It's not always easy to turn these temper tantrum episodes into learning moments. And of course, tantrums also vary from child to child. For some children, tantrums are a full blown blast, while for others they are just a gentle breeze.

Ed and Susan's son, Giles, and daughter, Bessy, exhibited two quite different cases of tamper tantrums. Giles, their first born, was an easy case of the terrible twos. His occasional tantrums were usually brief and often had obvious reasons. One instance was when Ed took his family with him on a business trip to Washington DC. Ed's colleagues invited Ed's family for lunch at a very nice cafe inside a mall. They all settled down and started ordering food. As soon as Giles, two and half years old, was off from his stroller, he zoomed through people as if he had a specific destination in mind. Determined, he was. His parents took turns stopping him in his track. They were afraid he could get hurt or lost in such a crowded place. The little gentleman got all upset every time his parents stopped him and brought him back to the restaurant table.

"Giles, you need to stay with us here. You're gonna have an accident; there are so many people here, see," his father told him pointing to all the people going around them.

Giles, however, kept on saying, *"Wada, wada!.."* Every time Ed took him back, he got increasingly upset until he threw a serious tantrum. He kept on repeating *"Wada, wada!.."* while pointing in the direction to which he was running. At that point Ed and Susan hadn't realized that their son was running toward a fountain located a couple of feet from their table. Giles loved playing in water; it was one of his favorite activities. *"Wada, wada!.. "* meant "water, water..." Since he didn't often have tantrums, his father decided to let him go and followed behind. Giles went straight up to the fountain! As soon as he got to the fountain (which probably reminded him of his bathtub at home), the little guy got ready to jump in! His father caught him just in the nick of time as Giles was climbing on the concrete bench around the fountain and was about to jump into the water. His father explained to him that that place wasn't made for swimming, but to no avail. Giles got even more upset and picked up his tantrum where he had left it. Despite many onlookers' stares, Ed kept his calm and focused on calming his son. He sat holding Giles by the fountain. After a while, Giles somewhat started to calm down, and his attention went to something else. Slowly, his tantrum eased off. How much did Giles understand what his father was trying to explain to him, that he couldn't just jump into the fountain? One cannot tell. But one thing for sure helped Giles' father address his son's tantrum: he was able to know the reason behind his son's frustration.

Some tantrums, however, don't seem to have any reasons at all. And those are the most challenging ones to address as this happened with Ed and Susan's daughter, Bessy. She was a classic temper tantrum thrower, and quite the opposite of her brother Giles. Even though Susan ignored her daughter's carrying-on, it took Bessy longer to get hold of herself and calm down. Needless to say, it took tons of patience on Susan's part to keep her cool and go about other business as if her daughter's acting out didn't bother her. Susan always spoke first with her daughter before "ignoring" her tantrums.

"I know you are angry, and you feel like crying. That's OK. If you want to cry, that's OK too. How long do you want to cry, two or three minutes?" Susan showed her two, then three fingers.

When Bessy was very little, around two or three, and was learning how to let her "magic inside" help her calm down, she always chose more time, i.e., three minutes. Almost always she stopped before half that time! She would refuse to go on when her mother reminded her that she still had more time to cry. No matter what Bessy did during the time that *she* chose, Susan completely tuned out.

What Susan found out was that this ignoring approach, discussed earlier, worked better for both her and her daughter. Bessy knew that her mother wouldn't stop her from crying. Instead, she welcomed it. She gave her daughter time to dwell on her frustrations. At the same time, Susan kept her sanity by knowing that there would be an end to it all -- which sometimes felt like it would never come! Later, Bessy eventually learned how to let go of her anguish after she had the time to go through it. When Bessy calmed down, Susan usually spoke with her about what had happened. Some days were easier than others. The insecurity of being unable to articulate her frustration, feeling powerless to do what she wanted to led Bessy to what she *could* do to express herself, i.e., tantrums.

Just as Susan did after Bessy had calmed down from her tantrums, we need to discuss with our child what happened. Above all, we have to reassure our child that we love her and that her being frustrated is legitimate, i.e., validate her frustrations. In doing so, we increase our odds of addressing our child's frustrations and/or complaints much more effectively.

Addressing A Child's Complaints

All children complain at one time or another. Empathizing with his feelings of discomfort can help alleviate his frustration of not being understood. As stated earlier, sometimes children cannot articulate their problems, and they therefore whine to attract attention without explaining why or what is the problem. In some cases, we unbeknowingly foster this situation by readily running to the child every time he whines so that we can fix whatever he is whining about. As we do so, consciously or unconsciously, we are allowing and reinforcing our child to think that it is all right to whine and not appropriately express himself to get help in solving his problems. One of the effective ways to help him address his problems is through *paraphrasing* what he's trying to tell us. This can be a real catalyst in appropriately helping him articulate his frustrations.

"I see that you and your friend Ryan are having problems playing together with your toys today. What happened?" Julie asks her three year old son Sean when he runs to her from the sand-box in the park where Sean has been playing with his friend Ryan.

As a matter of fact, it is usually unwise to concentrate on "*Why* did you do this, or say this or that, or behave this way or that way?" Because it is actually his inability to express herself, to articulate what he is feeling, that brings about the whining in the first place. And asking him to do just what has frustrated him in the first place makes him more so upset. We may also wind up getting frustrated because we may think that he doesn't really want to tell us what is bothering him!

The following scenario is somewhat similar to that with Bessy and her mother Susan, but with much more insight on the child being able to articulate her frustration(s). This is about Kenny and his three year old daughter Molly. In the beginning, Kenny put his daughter in "time-out" to calm her down when she started endless whining leading to tantrums. Molly used to carry on for what seemed like forever, Kenny said. During this time, Kenny was very tempted to speak with his daughter, to plead with her, or at least to tell her to STOP the drama! But as his daughter realized that her father did not pay any attention to her until she calmed down, she started whining less and less. When she calmed down, her father was able to pay better attention to her. That way, Kenny said, he was able to respond better to his daughter's needs and/or demands. There were also times, Kenny remarked, when his daughter told him that she didn't know why she felt restless and upset. Those were the most challenging times to be patient with his daughter. When Kenny inadequately and repeatedly asked his daughter, " Why are you crying?" Molly would sometimes say, "Daddy, I don't know why... I just wanna cry!" For a three year old child, that's as good an explanation as it can get. In such instances, Kenny would only comfort his daughter by holding her or letting her calm down at their chosen "quiet down place."

The above scenarios portray situations when a child is in his home environment, with his parents. What happens when a child goes to school and has complaints, sometimes valid, about his teachers or the school? What do we do to help our child? As stated earlier, children complain now and then without any serious cause. However, when a youngster constantly complains about his teachers, for instance, to the point that he cannot interact and function appropriately, and if he even becomes apprehensive about going to school, it is our obligation to address the situation *immediately*. We must pay attention to his complaints and see if they are well founded. If and when they are, or when in doubt, we have to request a meeting with the concerned teacher(s). Our goal is to help the child, i.e., to work *with* his teacher(s) to see how the problem situation can be remedied in the child's best interest.

Times have changed a lot from our generation when we were children. My father's motto, "The teacher is always right," for instance, doesn't often work in the child's best interest these days. If and when we know that our child has a problem with discipline, i.e., following family rules and regulations at home, chances are that he is more likely to have the same problem at school. Belittling the child's complaints and frustrations or blowing them out of proportion is also counterproductive. It's our responsibility to find ways to teach him how to respect authority and follow school rules and regulations while remaining assertive of his own needs.

Equally important is not to be critical of the teacher(s) or the child without *first* getting all the information. We cannot help our child when we are overwhelmed with emotions and jump to conclusions and start calling his teacher names, in front of the child. We have the responsibility to teach and help our youngster understand that all teachers are not the same. Some are friendlier than others, some are more upbeat than others, and some are more patient than others. This is an important life lesson in and of itself. We are teaching him that throughout life he will come into contact, work, and interact with people who will not necessarily be pleasant to him, reasonable, or sympathetic to his cause. He must eventually learn how he can over-look some of people's personality issues and effec-tively address what needs to be done without necessarily starting a world war.

As much as addressing complaints is a challenge, addressing our child's lies is even a greater challenge. *Lying* leads to a breach of trust within the parent-child relationship. The situation is not as serious with younger children as it is with older children who be-come sophisticated in their deceit.

LYING

There are lies and lies. Everyone, at some point in their life, has told a lie of some sort. A great many peo-ple, at one time or another, have told "white" lies. These lies are told to save face or avoid hurting other people's feelings. Small children are unsophisticated when they tell a lie to save face. When three year old Suzie takes a spoonful of sugar that her mom told her not to, then says she didn't eat any while she still has sugar all over her mouth, that's a little lie to save face. It becomes another story when she becomes sophisti-cated in hiding the evidence.

Parents need to be concerned when these occasional lies become *chronic*. By the age of five or so, if a child still does not have any sense of right and wrong and lies or steals without guilt or remorse, professional help is more than recommended. It is alarming when at the age of five or so, a child hasn't developed yet any sense of right or wrong through a loving, trusting relationship with at least one parent/caretaker. These emotional problems get more difficult to remedy the older the child gets. It's very important that parents, through their own examples, make it clear to their child that lying as well as stealing is not acceptable.

Cheating is another form of lying. If he cheats at school, for instance, we have to make it clear that it's not only unacceptable but also wrong to do so. We need to make him accountable for his actions. *He* must tell the teacher that he didn't do his own report or assignment, for instance, and let him live with the consequences. Cheating can be benign when it's an isolated incident. Nonetheless, it must be made clear to the child that, however insignificant the situation may be, it is still unacceptable behavior. As stated before, if the cheating and lying turn into a habit, it becomes a problem that must be addressed.

ADDRESSING LYING

When we realize that our child repeatedly lies, we need to first look at what we parents do in that regard. Are we setting good examples when it comes to telling the truth? When we tell other people things that we and *he* know are not true, when we tell him to say something untrue to other people to save *our* "integrity," we are, consciously or unconsciously, creating confusion in his mind.

When we find out that our child cheated in his tests at school, for instance, let's first ask ourselves the reasons why he felt that he had to cheat. Is it that he didn't study? Is it because we put so much emphasis on better grades regardless of how he goes about getting them? Or is it the teacher, the school? If in our interactions with the child we made it clear that cheating is not acceptable, he is usually embarrassed after he is caught cheating. He is more likely to show remorse or embarrassment. Showing appropriate remorse is, in a way, a sign of his self-analysis -- and <u>not</u> low self-esteem.

We are constant models to our child. "Do as I say, not as I do" doesn't work in the long run. Children are our best copy cats. They will, in the end, most likely do as *we* do, especially when they enter into their adolescence years.

TEEN YEARS: ADOLESCENT BEHAVIOR

Puberty stricken youngsters undergo physical, emotional, social, and even spiritual changes at a very fast pace. There are various myths and realities about teenagers. One of these myths is that *all* youngsters in this phase are rebellious, that adolescence is synonymous with rebellion; rebellion against all for which their parents stand or represent. For some youngsters, adolescence is a hurricane period which seems to never end! As soon as he thinks that he has an aspect of his life under control, another one pops up. He has to do another adjustment process all over again: stress and anxiety of the unknown, surprises, new responsibilities. *His* reality is that the turmoil of these changes will *never* end. Is it any wonder that adolescents seem "crazy!"

However, not *all* teenagers are "crazy." I rather prefer to call them the yet "mal-adjusted," if such a word exists. His adjustment and re-adjustments depend on various factors, such as personality, information on what's happening to his body and psyche, degree of parental support, family contexts and circumstances. One factor stands out as to how well or ill adjusted a youngster faces these new challenges of adolescence: how well informed or mis-informed he is about what he is going through. In cultures with programs and rituals that give structure to the transition from childhood to adulthood, cases of adolescents' total rebellion are negligible. The long period of a child's dependence on his parents is somewhat shortened by these rites of passage to adulthood.

Parents know from experience that, however dramatic and long it may *feel*, this life episode shall also pass. Their support and guidance help provide their out-of-balance adolescent with skills on how to cope with and adjust to these physical and emotional changes within and without. The critical challenge here for us is to teach him the skills he needs to know how to *think* before acting out on his feelings, however legitimate these feelings may be. Thinking enables him to pause and make appropriate choices despite his drive for instant gratification.

How then can we help him learn to control his right-now-feel-good inclination for a greater, lasting sense of accomplishment and satisfaction in the long run? No one has an adolescent-proof answer to this question...yet. The good news is that there is a number of techniques that can motivate an adolescent to think and make wise choices for himself. The best available approach, as explained throughout this book, is *walking the talk*, i.e., being role models in all aspects of life to our child. Above all, it is unwise and counterproductive to pretend with our youngster that we know *everything* about life. The experience we had growing up, even though of great help, is still *our* experience. Even though some truths about life never change, our child's reality is most likely to differ from ours.

We can effectively help give direction to our child when we *tune into* his reality. Not as it *should* be, but *as it is*. This doesn't mean that we condone the *status quo* of his reality, but that we get in a better position to help when we go from how things really are for him.

At the same time, we also have to learn not to become too understanding of our adolescent as this may backfire in the end. Furthermore, we have to expect that, at one time or another, he *will* have quite angry and hostile feelings toward us. This goes for good as well as poor parents. To make avoiding his anger towards us our ultimate parenting goal is running on empty. This anger is going to happen, especially when we appropriately and effectively play our ultimate role of regulator, educator, and teacher. Almost every child goes through these feelings of ambivalence, i.e., love and hate toward us. It's normal ... to a certain degree.

We have, by all means, to share with our adolescent our opinions concerning his behavior. Discussing our feelings with him is, however, completely different from insisting that he accept them as his own without question. When he does something of which we disapprove, we need to discuss with him not only his behavior *per se*, but also how his behavior puts him at greater risk for getting hurt. It's not unusual, at one time or another, for an adolescent to ignore or even reject his parents' advice and do the opposite of what they expect of him. Sometimes the school of hard knocks can be the best way for our child to learn life's realities. We have, nonetheless, to make clear that we care about his safety although it is basically his choice. We love him, and we are concerned for his well-being even when we don't approve of his choices. Actually, adolescent children don't very much care what we think until they think that we care! We need to learn to be open for discussion about anything that our adolescent brings up. We are in a better position to conduct more logical, reasonable, and constructive discussions with our *illogical* youngster when we are aware of the realities of the era in which he lives. Even when these discussions do not change anything, they are nonetheless necessary to eventually awaken logical thinking in his *rebellious* state of mind.

ADOLESCENCE "REBELLION"

Adolescent children want to assert themselves, to affirm their own persons to the point that they may start, given their inexperience, immaturity, and *naiveté*, getting in trouble again and again because of the choices they make. Regardless, we have to continue to provide them with a model of how to *constructively* assert themselves. Our adolescent child needs our support more than ever when he wants to break away. We play, as mentioned earlier, the dual role of both *facilitators* (helping him assert his individuality) and *regulators* (teaching him the social boundaries for his behavior).

He may come to believe that to affirm his independence also means to test how far he can push us around. He may start to order his parents around and pester them to the point that some of us would rather just let him do whatever he wants so long as he leaves us in peace. Unfortunately, inappropriately giving in to a child (because we can't take the nagging and pestering any longer) gives way to inconsistency and the crumbling of the family anchor.

We also have to respond to a child's behavior and demands with *common sense*. To reasonably teach him how to be accountable for his decisions, we have to find an appropriate balance between offense and penalty. As with everything else in life, moderation is a good guide. The severity of a penalty must be related to the magnitude of his misbehavior. The penalty mustn't be so harsh that it devastates his morale. On the other hand, it mustn't be so insignificant that he doesn't make any effort to modify his unwanted behavior.

We, the adults, have to find the right measure between how to teach our adolescent child acceptable behavior AND learn to know when a rebellious attitude can be a good thing for him. Flexibility, discussed in chapter two, is of the utmost importance here. A child who complies with every one of his parents' wishes may wind up living his life only to fulfill his parent's wishes and not *his*.

At a bereavement support group, I once met a gentleman, Mark, who was a full blown case of a "totally obedient" child. A parent's dream child, right? Well, Mark never married, never had lasting friends. He broke up with his true love, because Rosie, his widowed mother, didn't approve. As a matter of fact, Rosie didn't approve of any of the girls that her son dated and wanted to marry. From her standpoint, the girls were not good enough. Mark, an only child, wound up spending his life as a lonely man. He was in his late forties when his mother passed away. He then found himself in extreme rage at his dead mother. He was trying to come to terms with why he complied with *all* his mother's wishes to the extent that he didn't really start to live *his* own life until then. He was learning how to live *on his own* in his late forties!

Common sense and flexibility within family dynamics enable parents to learn to know when their child needs them and when he needs his space. There are, however, cases of teen rebellion that fall out of the norm. For such cases, professional help would be the best alternative. Sometimes, it just happens that the best parents on earth may wind up having terrible children, and the lousiest parents get terrific children!

A child's disobedience or defiance needn't always be considered a sign of emotional turmoil. We have to expect and accept it and take the opportunity to help him manage his defiance constructively. His defiance may be a process in constructively defining his own place in the world.

Usually, when a child's needs for affection, attention, acceptance, approval, and support have been appropriately met by the significant persons in his life, be it his parents, grandparents, or any other primary caregivers, disobedience and acts of total defiance are minimal. When a child's feelings are respected, when he is not belittled for making mistakes or for his efforts, he learns to care about other persons' feelings. He is more likely to look at his family rules and regulations as protection and support instead of deprivation and unfair punishment.

As said earlier, we do make mistakes in the process of raising our child responsibly. We don't jeopardize our child's respect for us when we fully acknowledge our mistakes. We are neither *belittled* nor *reduced* in our child's eyes. Being honest about ourselves teaches humility. He learns *from us* that it's OK to make mistakes as long as we own up to them and learn from them. We are *not* the *superhuman people* he might have once thought we were. Being an adequate parent is a truly humbling experience in every way.

An effective alternative to dealing with our adolescent child's inappropriate behavior or problems is to address them. Ignoring or avoiding important issues doesn't make them go away. They get bigger and bigger, and before we know it, they blow up in our face. Putting up with unacceptable behavior, even if we think we deserve such treatment, does not change the fact that there is always a limit to what a person can tolerate, however patient that person may be. Furthermore, by always putting up with unacceptable behavior because "it's only a phase he is going through," we are *confirming* to the youngster that unacceptable behavior *can be* acceptable!

Nora was a very well-mannered, collected, young girl in her early teens. Two years after her mother sent her to live with her great aunt, Brenda, she started to hang out with what's termed the "wrong crowd." Her behavior started to change; she started to be "fresh" with her great aunt. Brenda had raised four children of her own. They were all grown and out in the world when Nora came to live with her. When Brenda was raising her children, she always wanted to know with whom her children socialized. Brenda decided to meet with Deidra, Sally's mother, when Nora started hanging out with Sally. Sally treated Deidra with disrespect, even in front of her friends. After she met with Deidra, Brenda somewhat understood Sally's obnoxiousness toward her mother and the changes in her grand niece's behavior toward her. She decided to have a serious talk with Nora. The latter told her that she didn't really want to disrespect her, but that she was very upset because her mom had not been able to keep her. Brenda explained to Nora that she had the right to be upset about what had happened to her. Anytime she felt like talking about this or any other issue, she, Brenda, was there for her. However, Brenda told Nora that she, Nora, could not for a second use what happened to her as an excuse for not doing the right thing. Brenda made it then very clear to Nora that rudeness or disrespect would no longer be tolerated.

Brenda cleared up her problem situation with her grand niece, a situation that many of us sometimes do not have the courage to address with our hormonally challenged children. We need to explain to our child that grown-ups can and do also have their feelings hurt when he uses hurtful words toward us. The sooner a child learns about it, the more likely he will understand that people, small or big, want to be treated as kindly as he does.

The kind of relationship that exists between parents and a child in his early years plays an important role in his adolescence years. To the extent that this early parent-child relationship was constructive and supportive, even though an adolescent child may seem at times like a total stranger, he will more likely care about his parents' opinions, reactions, feelings, and moral precepts. However, regardless of how adequate or inadequate that early parent-child relationship has been, if it seems too late for parents to help the child, for heaven's sake, seek appropriate professional help. The Colombine massacre in 2000 that shook every parent around the nation is but one instance of adolescents' extreme crises. It is hard to believe these children's parents missed all the warning signs of serious trouble-in-waiting through their children's behaviors years before that nightmare.

On a brighter note, many adolescents overcome their turmoil and develop into responsible, maturing teenagers. They become capable of handling family responsibilities and other challenges that their parents entrust them with. They get a profound sense of accomplishment, self-esteem, and a belief that they *are* indeed important members of their family through their contribution to their family dynamics. This can be heightened by parents who acknowledge and appreciate their children's efforts and valuable help in the family.

However well-adjusted our youngster may be when he enters his adolescent years, he will, at one time or another, have deceptive behavior, this being an integral part of growing up.

DECEPTIVE BEHAVIORS

Deceptive behavior in adolescence has almost the same causes as those in early childhood, only they become much more sophisticated. How can we address these problematic situations with our adolescent child?

Adolescent children very much want to be considered as grown-ups and independent. They behave as if they don't need any advice, especially from their parents. They know "everything." However, the degree to which they go on blowing one responsibility after another speaks for itself: they still need their parents' guidance and wisdom. When your adolescent child is out of line and still adopts a know-it-all attitude, it's not easy to stay calm and take time to teach him what is acceptable and constructive behavior. This is more than ever the time he needs structure, loving support, and guidance the most. Even though there may be times when he rejects some family values as a way of "breaking away" from his family, we still have to provide him with examples of how to act responsibly. At other times, as hard as it might be, we need to confront him.

As mentioned earlier, getting angry and constructively expressing it is not only healthy but also beneficial to both the child and the parent. By constructively expressing our anger, we convey a message to him that one can get angry with what a loved one did and still cherish that person. If people who love each other and live together don't *ever* get angry, or at least frustrated with each other, such a relationship is either one sided or a very superficial one. We don't need to argue all the time to prove our closeness, but we need to be *secure enough* of our closeness that we don't need to approve or like everything the other does. Our task is to teach and provide him with examples of a healthy relationship from a very young age: he doesn't have to be afraid of losing our love and support because he gets angry at us or voices his opinions (opinions that may be completely different from ours), or when we penalize him for his wrong doing.

WHEN PUNISHMENT IS NECESSARY

As much as parents need to minimize punishment or withholding of privileges, they needn't avoid it at all cost. In some situations, as stated earlier, children are better off learning from the school of hard knocks. Corrective punishment can range from light penalties such as not playing video games for a certain number of hours or days to much more serious penalties such as complete loss of driving privileges and grounding. Effective punishments must be timely, fair, clear, and agreed on before a rule is broken as explained in chapter four. Otherwise punishment becomes a power struggle and a way to get back at a child for the inconveniences he causes. Once a penalty has been discussed and spelled out beforehand, preferably during family discussions, we are in the position to enforce that penalty when necessary. In such situations, there is less, conscious or unconscious, manipulation either by the parents or by the youngster.

Enforcing rules and administering penalties create all sorts of emotions, often those of animosity. Some of us fear that our child will no longer like us if and when we put restrictions on his activities. In the short run, this is most likely to happen; he *will* dislike us because of these boundaries. Nevertheless, down the road, he may eventually come to have deep respect and consideration for his parents' courage in setting reasonable limits on his behavior. When there is a system or structure in place, a child most likely knows beforehand what to expect when he breaks a rule. He is not likely to resent his penalty as much as if he didn't know what's coming to him.

Let me make this clear here: punishment is recommended as of last resort for behavior modification, and not an ongoing, routine way to discipline a child. We must constantly use the more *positive* forms of discipline, i.e., praise, persuasion, reasoning, and rewarding so that when punishment is what a child deserves, that's then what he will get.

When punishment is administered, it must be *immediately* after the misbehavior or misdeed, or immediately after we learn about it. When punishment is too far removed from the misdeed, it doesn't usually have the same effect as when it is immediately administered. The child doesn't probably make any clear connection between what he did (or didn't do) and the punishment, especially when the child is still very young. He may not even remember what he did. We have to be as explicit as possible when explaining to a child about his offense and making it clear to *him* why he's being penalized. The ultimate goal for penalties is to promote his healthy self-criticism so that he learns to be accountable for his own decisions and thus self-regulate responsibly.

Children's reactions to punishment are very different from one child to another, and we have to adjust penalties accordingly. Let's also make sure that we don't punish him twice for the same offense. If one of the parents, for instance, already punished the child, the other must refrain from punishing him again. And other times, the natural consequences of his actions are the best penalty for him.

NATURAL CONSEQUENCES

According to *Families Anonymous*, letting a child live the consequences of his own decisions and actions is referred to as "tough love." It's a hard, tough way for him to learn about some facts of life. But it sure works!

Terri's oldest son, Matt, is but one example of adolescent youngsters who eventually learn the hard way. Matt, an eighteen year old high school senior could legally drive in the state of Georgia. Terri, a divorced mother raising her two boys on her own, decided to let Matt use her car on weekends, mostly to drive to his weekend job. Sometimes Terri let her son use the car for some special occasions such as going to a party or to the movies with friends. Matt wanted to buy a car. However, Terri wanted him to save his money for college instead. She explained to her son the advantages and shortcomings of using his savings to buy a used car during his senior year. He would, she explained to him, probably wind up spending all his money on car insurance, repairs, gas, even though it seemed it would be easier for him to get around if he bought a car. Instead of buying a car, Terri told her son that she would let him use her car as long as he used it responsibly.

After a while, however, Matt started to abuse this privilege by using his mother's vehicle for purposes other than those he and his mother agreed on. One day, Terri decided to test her son's trustworthiness in this regard. Unbeknownst to Matt, Terri wrote down the mileage before her son left, supposedly for his weekend job which was located about two miles from their home. When her son came back that night, Terri checked the odometer. Matt had put on more than 35 miles for a distance that should have been at the most 5 or 6 miles! Terri asked her son how that could be? Matt's explanation didn't hold, and above all, he didn't even apologize for abusing his mother's trust. Terri took away that privilege from her son right there and then. A couple of months later, without his mother's approval, Matt decided to buy his own car -- a used car. He spent most of his savings on insurance and car repairs. After a little over ten months or so, his car died, leaving him with next to nothing in savings. He had to work even harder to pay for college because Terri didn't lay out the money, which she was going to do if Matt had kept his end of the bargain. A little over a year later, the same scenario repeated itself with Ron, Terri's second son!

Grounding penalties, i.e., being confined to the house for a given number of days, can also be an effective approach to penalize an adolescent child who is out of line. When verbal warnings have been overlooked, grounding may prove to be effective when appropriately administered. When our youngster commits an offense which can be remedied, the best approach would be to have him rectify what he did, i.e., *restitution.*

RESTITUTION

When and if possible, an act of *restitution* is a form

of penalty that's rather altruistic. It develops a sense of caring about other people's feelings and teaches the child to put himself in another person's shoes. When, for instance, Carolyn breaks down her brother Sam's *Lego* castle because he wouldn't let her play with it, this is an opportunity to teach her that what she's done is unacceptable. She has to rebuild the *Lego* castle AND apologize to her brother. Rebuilding the castle, in this case, teaches Carolyn that she must correct her misdeed (destroying her brother's toy) and thereby lessen the pain she caused him.

Many parents today have embraced the "don't judge" pop psyche philosophy. I disagree with this philosophy. Here's a short reason why. Children, that is *all* children, even those who are easy to influence, are born *uncivilized.* I have yet to meet a child who is born completely well-adjusted to his environment from day one. Everyone must learn acceptable behavior. Learning acceptable behavior inevitably requires criticism, i.e., judging. *Positive* and *constructive* criticism that is. Such criticism eventually enables problem resolution within family dynamics.

PARENT-CHILD CONFLICT RESOLUTION

Problems are the very essence of life. They come up in any and every relationship, even in one as special as that of parent and child. It has always been so since the beginning of time. Conflicts spring up in the normal, healthy, course of daily interactions among family members. However, some conflicts may become more prevalent because of a particular chosen discipline approach that goes to extremes, either too strict or too permissive as mentioned in previous chapters. Conflicts are typically magnified when a child gets into his puberty years. How do we then go about addressing and resolving these conflict situations and preserving harmony within our parent-child relationship?

Many conflicts unfortunately end up in *quarrels* and *fault-finding* rather than in search of appropriate solutions. Parent, who are the adults, are in a better position to teach how to conduct a conflict resolution discussion much more constructively and logically. This is not particularly easy because children tend to be *illogical*. A constructive discussion where the goal is to find solutions without the intense emotions of hostility, shame, and resentment that are present in a quarrel is a viable and excellent venue (a quarrel is often started with the "I-told-you-so" tone that we sometimes take when a youngster gets in trouble). Therefore, *cooperation*, *mutual trust*, and *accountability* must be the ingredients of a parent-child discussion about conflict.

Active listening is a communication technique through which we listen to our child's viewpoint about things without a preconceived agenda. Active listening enables us to look for solutions to problems *along with* our youngster. Active listening rather than defensive listening is more likely to help create an atmosphere in which each side comes to the table with open minds rather than with a know-it-all stand. We have to set an example of how to speak *assertively* yet *kindly*, if not every time, at least most of the time creating therefore a *win-win* situation.

Making *compromises* in which each party gives up some of their demands usually brings about lasting solutions. When we foster an atmosphere of seeking mutually acceptable solutions when appropriate, our youngster may eventually learn to do the same in his interpersonal conflicts. If during our conflict discussion, we realize that we wronged our child, we would fare better when we acknowledge it right away and apologize to the child. In a way, this goes hand in hand with self-esteem. He learns that it's OK to have short-comings, and that owning up to them can make one even more so confident as he learns how to face them and eventually learn from them.

Summary

Our ultimate goal for behavior crisis management and conflict resolution is not to become our child's "best friend" or solve for him *all* his problems. We don't have to obsess about being his buddy, or getting his approval, at the cost of *robbing him of a parent*, something that he needs the most during his adolescent years. This *sacred* role of being a parent comes above everything else. Our adolescent child still needs his parents to guide him into becoming a well-rounded in-dividual by appropriately taking on his responsibilities, which is the topic of our next and last chapter.

Leading By Example Is Not A New Trend
(Author: Unknown)

Around the time of the Revolutionary War,
a squad of soldiers was struggling to move a piece of
heavy timber to build a fortification.
Supervising them was a smart-looking corporal
who was officiously instructing the men to "heave!"
But the effort proved futile.
The squad was not able to shift the timber enough.

A rider happened to pass by and quietly watched the operation.
He watched for a while and then said to the officer in charge:
"Why don't you help those men?"
"Who, me, sir? I'm a corporal."

The quiet stranger dismounted his horse and
took a place alongside the struggling soldiers.
"Now, all together lads, heave!"
With the extra muscle, the
timber was moved into place.

The man climbed back on his horse and said,
"Corporal, in the future when you have timber to move,
send for the commander-in-chief."

At that point the soldiers realized that
the helpful stranger was none other
than George Washington.

152

Chapter 6

On Responsibilities

"Seeing is better than hearing."
(African Proverb)

Routine Responsibilities

We may start, from a very early age, to teach our child about being responsible and learn to resist the urge to pick up after her. Family dynamics include daily activities, weekly or monthly discussion meetings, holiday celebrations, and family vacations. Daily activities and responsibilities include c*hores,* which can be as simple as a child learning to put her toys back in the toy box after she plays with them. This can be taught as a fun game between the child and the parent. When she is around three or four, deciding with her where to put her toys, may be an efficient way to help her form appropriate organizational habits. As we involve our child in the decision-making process about organizing things, this not only provides her with organizational skills but also fosters cooperation and responsibility among family members.

Being organized doesn't mean, however, that her things, or our home for that matter, have to be neat *all the time.* Doing it *as often as possible* is reasonable and realistic enough a goal to teach her a sense of order. Keeping things well organized around the house may not be among the most important skills that some of us may want to teach our child. And that's OK. There are so many other ways through which parents can teach their child about responsibilities, such as taking care of pets, watering plants, setting the table for dinner, putting dishes in the dishwasher, cooking dinner, or keeping an eye on a younger sibling.

Children don't always do their chores wholeheartedly. On some days, she will need more prompting than on others. We have to be prepared and even expect that there *will* be times when she will complain and resist doing her chores. It's unrealistic to think that she will enjoy raking the yard, for instance, or doing wholeheartedly her school homework *every day*.

Speaking of homework, our responsibility is to help her set a routine for doing homework, ideally one that is compatible with her other after-school activities. When she needs help with her homework, it is our responsibility to provide it to her. It is, however, not in her best interest that we do it for her because she is not in the mood to do it herself or we are afraid she will lag in her academics.

Daily, weekly, monthly chores, and other responsibilities must take into account her age, personality, situation, and context. The simpler and clearer these daily chores are, the more a child is likely to perform them without fuss. Weekly chores may, for instance, consist of doing the recycling, raking the yard, vacuuming bedrooms, or cleaning the bathroom. Making a *real* contribution gives her a sense that her family needs her, that *she* counts. Her parents' attitude and enthusiasm toward her contribution is crucial to her cooperative participation in household chores.

"Gee, look at what *I* can do all by myself,

mommy!" says four year old Kevin to his mom, Monica, after he puts his toys on a higher shelf of his toy closet.

With a big grin on her face, Monica ruffles her son's hair while saying, "Good job, excellent, buddy! Am I proud of you or what!" Monica's words of appreciation can but reinforce her son's sense of "can-do" attitude, self-esteem, and earned pride. Words of appreciation are powerful and persuasive in getting a child to keep up her end of the bargain; nagging or negative criticism are not.

Coming up with a *chore chart* may prove helpful. A chart for *daily chores* could be modified periodically throughout the year, while a *weekly* one for house cleaning, for instance, could be modified every week to allow each family member to get a chance at doing different chores -- especially in a family with multiple children. Modifying the chore chart periodically conveys a sense of fairness as children don't feel stuck in the same chores which may be harder than those for which their siblings are responsible. We have to remember here that, even if chores are relatively similar, rotation is always a sign of fairness since the "grass is always greener on the other side." Obviously, chores for older children ought to be relatively challenging compared to those for younger ones.

OLDER VS. YOUNGER SIBLINGS

In a family with multiple children, older children would be expected to help out with their younger siblings. We have to balance, however, our expectations by seeing to it that our older child left in charge actually has the skills and maturity to assume such an important responsibility. Making such a demand must be done in a way that enhances the older child's sense of pride and self-esteem. She may, eventually, come to see such a responsibility as a sign of her parents' trust and confidence in her.

Some of us prefer to give our older child money (as opposed to non-monetary incentives) as an incentive for baby-sitting for her younger sibling(s). That is OK. After all, she's starting to learn how to earn money and be trained in baby-sitting -- and may do this outside the home. Family members routinely do things for each other without any expectation of monetary or material rewards in return. It becomes a whole different situation when she refuses to do chores around the house unless she gets paid. A child who is paid for completing *routine* chores doesn't, in all likelihood, learn about being altruistic toward loved ones. Sharing responsibilities, fairly and appropriately, within a family reinforces family bonds and provides a child with a positive model about being of service to other people.

As important as family responsibilities are in boosting her sense of self-esteem, they have the potential of becoming detrimental when they drastically limit her social activities with her friends and peers, or restrict her time just to be by herself. Taking care of younger siblings must not be overwhelming to the point that the older child literally takes over her parents' parenting responsibility toward her younger siblings. This can lead to justified resentment toward her parents and, especially, her younger sibling(s). She understandably builds resentment for curtailing her time to do her own thing. She has her own life to live.

Children develop a sense of accountability through their active participation in family activities. Teaching a child about responsibilities actually compels her to focus, prioritize, organize, and think before acting out on her impulses. When she gets into adolescence, she is more likely to responsibly face issues as touchy as sex, drugs, and alcohol.

SEX EDUCATION RESPONSIBILITIES

Sexuality is a part of growing cannot up. It is real and cannon be ignored. Children need to be taught about responsibility in regard to sexual activities. Sex is a private and intimate act between two responsible, *consenting*, preferably married, *adults*. Making love, i.e., having sex, is an act that brings human beings to the instinctive, carnal, animal level, so to speak. This is a subject that is understandably uncomfortable to talk about. And the last person on earth with whom we want to talk about it is our child. Instinctively, we tend to keep this fact of life in a box.

But, in today's sexually permissive world, we cannot afford to kept *it* in the box. The earlier in life we take on this responsibility vis-à-vis our child, the better prepared she will be. Let's face it: if she doesn't get information from us, she *will* get it some other place. Molesters usually pick on children they know are vulnerable to begin with: children from broken homes, or children with no or ambiguous information about sex. Innocence hurts more than it helps in this regard. The danger of allowing our child to get misleading information "out there" far outweighs the discomfort we might feel about discussing sex with her. The earlier we start explaining the "birds and the bees" to her, the less uncomfortable the process of discussing this delicate issue when we need to engage in such discussions later on. A child who is appropriately informed about sex has a better chance of avoiding sexual abuse and premature sexual activities.

For a number of years, Rosalynn, a New York City social worker, worked at a center for troubled youth. She learned there how ignorance and wrong information made many of "her" children vulnerable to sexual molestation-- be it at home or out there. Some of these children became emotionally handicapped for the rest of their lives. When she had children of her own, two daughters and a son, she decided that she and her partner would be the ones to teach and provide inform to their children about sex -- before they even set foot in kindergarten.

One day Rosalynn overheard her five-year-old daughter Tina having a conversation with her nine year old cousin, Megan. Tina and Megan were sitting next to each other, in the back of Rosalynn's station wagon, chatting about various topics. Every now and then, Tina would call out to her mother to confirm what she was saying to her cousin. Rosalynn heard her daughter explain to Megan how she, Tina, came from her mom and daddy. She explained to Megan how her mommy and daddy loved each other very much and wanted to have her and her brother and sister. Her parents gave each a half of what would make her, Tina, whole, she said. These were all things that Rosalynn and her husband had explained to their daughters and son about their births. So far, so good. Then, suddenly, Tina asked:

"Mommy, how did Daddy's half met your half in your belly? How did Daddy put his half in your stomach?" And she turned to her cousin and proudly said, "Listen, after my Mommy explains to me, I'll explain to you." Then she sat back waiting for the answer.

As they were cruising on the Hudson River parkway on the Upper West Side of Manhattan in New York City, Rosalynn's first reaction was to tell her daughter at that moment, "No, not now Tina, I'm driving!" Then she realized that was exactly the kind of question she wanted her children to discuss with her. Usually, she took her time to calmly explain, and then ask if her kids had any other questions. But that was not quite feasible during the car ride. However, Rosalynn did manage to have the following exchange with her daughter.

"Tina, you know that Mommy and Daddy love each other very much, right?"

"Yeaah, I know that," Tina said rolling her eyes.

"Well, there are times when your Daddy and I want to spend some time, just the two of us, in private, right?"

"Yes, I know thaaaat!" Tina said rather annoyed.

"Sometimes, during these moments together by ourselves Daddy and Mommy get very close and Daddy puts his half inside Mommy to meet Mommy's half that made you! When we get home, I promise I'll explain it all to you; now I'm driving and have to pay attention to the road, otherwise we'll have an accident... I promise I'll explain to you as soon as we get home, O.K.?"

Tina then turned toward Megan and re-explained what her mother had just said to her, even though Megan heard the explanation. When they got home, Rosalynn reminded her daughter as she promised. Rosalynn started giving Megan a more detailed picture about her conception and birth: sperm coming from the penis and going through the vagina to meet the ovum. Rosalynn stopped as soon as Tina asked her in the middle of the conversation, "Mommy," Tina said, "Can we

159

go to the swimming pool please!"

In this example, Tina didn't hesitate to ask her Mom about sex, because her parents had discussed it in the home before. Rosalynn and her husband made it possible and easier for their daughters and son to come to them with questions. They were *askable* parents to their children as there were no taboo questions in their home. Explanations about sex or any other facts of life needn't be too scientific with complicated technical terms. Simple ones about body parts and their functions, for instance, are a good start to keeping the door to sex education open.

When we answer a child's questions honestly and directly, she is more likely to come back to us for more information. However, *overloading* her with too much, age-inappropriate information is of no help either. Her non-verbal cues are also as important as her verbal inquiries. When Tina tells her mother, "let's go out to the swimming pool," while her mother is still explaining heartily about her birth, that's Tina's way of saying, "Uh, that's enough for me, mother, please, time out... I don't know any more what you're talking about ...or that's more than what I needed from you, etc." We have to learn to know *how* and *when* we start overloading our child with information that is irrelevant to *her* at that moment.

As she gets into her adolescent years, our explanations about sex must also become more sophisticated. This is the time during which her hormones and sexual drives come into play. Our task is to provide her with information and make it clear that *she* is responsible for her sexual activities. Sex can be a wonderful thing when it's done at the *right time*, with the *right person*, and for the *right reason(s)*. Or it can be a *destructive* thing when it happens for the wrong reasons, with the wrong person, at the wrong time. While some parents want that their child wait until when she gets married to become sexually active, the reality is that it's just a *wish*. The youngster is better off if and when we explain to her ahead of time about the realities of her responsibility in regard to *dating* and sexual activities.

DATING AND SEXUAL RESPONSIBILITIES

It's in the best interest of both parents and most certainly their adolescent child to openly discuss dating and sexual activities. We have to set clear and reasonable expectations and limits on our child's dating activities. By this time in her life, she is already familiar with the basic values that matter the most to her family. Making a contract, *albeit* oral, in this regard, may be of great help. We also need to consider what her peers consider "normal" as well as the norms of the community in which we live, to better understand the issue from *her* perspective, so that we can responsibly guide her.

Considering what her peers are doing or find normal doesn't, in any way, mean that we must also condone whatever her friends are doing. It rather opens up the door to an effective, two-way communication through which we learn facts and realities of the time. Parents will then be in a position to help their child AND provide her with enough information to make informed decisions. Eventually, she will learn that sex comes with strings attached, i.e., responsibilities.

As much as sexual drives in adolescence are a reality, so are issues of drug and alcohol abuse. In fact, there's a positive relationship between drug and alcohol use and sex. Dating and sexual responsibilities also lead to financial responsibilities such as expenses for activities that a youngster may decide to do with her peers. Is it our responsibility to pick up all her tabs?

FINANCIAL RESPONSIBILITIES

The child's basic necessities of life, i.e., shelter, food, protection, must naturally be provided by the parents until she reaches a certain age when she slowly but steadily takes on these responsibilities. Another equally important parental obligation is to teach and discuss with our adolescent child how to earn and budget her money in order to get the things she *wants* and how she will go about *earning* her leisure money, be it from her allowance, after school work, or summer job. She will learn that as much as her parents are responsible for providing her with what she needs, the *extras* that her parents give, once in a while, are basically hers to earn on her own. The sooner she learns that her parents are neither her *maids* nor her *gold mine*, the better she will be at setting goals for herself on how she will go about being financially responsible.

Terri and her sons, Matt and Ron, from chapter five provide a good scenario on teaching our youngster how to learn to become financially responsible. We parents also have to learn the skills and tact to get our child's *cooperation* to be able to teach her the facts of living responsibly.

MOTIVATING A CHILD TO COOPERATE

Allowing children to participate in the discussions of family rules and regulations fosters their imagination, creativity, and eventually, critical thinking. As mentioned earlier, their input will more likely lead to getting their cooperation in effectively applying these rules. Most of the prerequisites for effective self-regulation, i.e., self-discipline discussed in chapter four, also lead to cooperation from children in taking on their responsibilities.

Other techniques such as prompting, suggesting, persuasion, verbal appeals, contracting, and positive group or peer pressure, are techniques that can motivate a child to cooperate. Again, as stated earlier, the effectiveness of a chosen family motivating system depends on the imperative that both children AND parents observe these chosen and agreed upon rules; it's a win-win, *two-way street*.

Two Way Street

How we interact with our child plays an important role in how she responds to our expectations. When we are helpful and sensitive to her needs, when we are as pleasant as possible to her, she is most likely to adopt the same attitude towards our expectations and demands. Sometimes our kids outsmart us in this regard. Have you ever seen when a youngster wants a favor from you? She finds ways to set you up, or "butter you up." She naturally wants to get you in a pleasant mood and then asks for a particular favor from you! Usually, people are much more cooperative when they are in a good mood.

Setting up or predisposing a child into cooperation consists of rewarding her for something she did or for a behavior she emulates before asking her to do something else.

"You can play with your dog for an extra thirty minutes, Amanda," says Perry to his daughter. "After that, please set the table for dinner, will you? Thank you."

The odds that Perry will get cooperation from his

daughter are much higher than if he'd asked Amanda to set up the dinner table right after she played with Flu-flu, the dog.

There are other ways to favorably predispose a child to our expectations and demands, the most influential one, as stressed throughout this book, is through our own example which the child will more likely be motivated to emulate.

PARENTS' EXAMPLE

By nature, small children usually want to *be like* their parents. They want to be considered "as big as daddy, or "as pretty as Mommy." They want to feel powerful and competent. They, therefore, want to do things that their significant adults do.

"See what I can do, Mommy... all by myself!" says three year-old Samantha, trying to tie her shoes.

"Look how I can feed baby Ned," says four year-old Doreen to her mom as she feeds her baby brother; "Just like you do it, Mommy!"

Setting up play dates, with children whose behavior is more likely to have a positive impact on our child is also helpful in reinforcing acceptable behavior. Positive peer pressure can be a powerful motivator to emulate acceptable behavior. During adolescence, techniques that appeal to emotions, such as persuasion and verbal appeals, may be more effective in persuading a youngster to do the right thing rather than nagging.

PROMPTING

Prompting, by which we assist our child by saying or suggesting a course of action she's supposed to perform but has forgotten to do, is also another way to help her remember what is expected of her in certain situations. Prompts can be either *verbal* or *nonverbal*.

Some examples of *verbal prompts* are listed below.

"What do you do after you play with your bike, Simon?" Matt asks his five-year-old son, reminding Simon therefore to put his bike back in the garage.

"I have to put it back in the garage, Daddy, remember?" says Simon giggling.

"What do we do before we cross the street, Bob?" Don asks his four-year-old son, to remind Bob about street safety.

"Look left... Look right... and look left... and look right... when it's all right ... then quickly cross the street," says Bob, humming to the tune that his Dad taught him.

"Melissa, remember at 8:30 p.m., what do we do?" Ted asks his five-year-old daughter Melissa, to remind her about ending all activities and going up to brush her teeth and get ready for bed.

Nonverbal prompts would be something like putting the index finger on the lips, for instance, which means, "Be quiet!"

Prompts, like orders, are more effective when they are given in a pleasant, friendly, non-embarrassing, and calm tone. Even though the child may know family routines, we cannot expect her to remember them on her own *all the time*.

Sometimes rendering situations more "visible" may help a child remember what is expected of her in certain situations. Appealing to a child's imagination and raising her curiosity through dialogue, for instance, are more effective alternatives than the logical explanation of reasons behind some facts of life. *Dramatizing* makes a fact of life much more vivid and *real* to the child, therefore more meaningful to *her*. We have, however, to make a distinction between dramatization and *exaggeration* of facts. The latter doesn't usually have lasting results as it carries strains of deception. As much as dramatizing helps tickle a child's imagination and her thinking process, presenting a number of alternatives through suggestions is even more effective as the child actively participates in the choices to be made.

SUGGESTING

Among different techniques to seek cooperation from a child, *suggesting* is far more likely to lead to effective, two-way communication -- especially with teenagers. Suggestions raise a youngster's thinking process. There is no direct pressure on her to comply with our suggestions. Acting or not acting on the suggestions is left up to her.

Suggestions can be *direct* or *indirect*. Direct suggestions work better with younger children, while indirect suggestions work better with older ones.

Direct:

"Would you rather buy this pair of shoes now at Mr. Expensive Brand Store and use up all your money," Pete asks his ten year old son Matthew as he drives him to the mall, "or buy a similar pair at Mr. Bargain Brand Store and save yourself some money that you'll use to buy the *ipod* you told me about?"

Here, Matthew has been, in subtle ways, given a course of action by his father: he either spends a lot of money for the expensive shoes and foregoes buying the *ipod*, or he buys the less, yet similar, reasonably priced shoes and saves money to buy the *ipod*. Pete leaves it up to Matthew.

With an indirect suggestion, parents don't lay down a course of action as they do in a direct one, but their suggestion merely initiates the thought process within the child.

Indirect:

"Jim is grounded, isn't he?" Marla speaks rather rhetorically to her seventeen year old son Mark about his best friend Jim. "What do you think about what Jim did when he used his parents' car for things other than what he promised them he would?" Marla asks Mark as the two of them head to the community center where Mark (and eighteen year old Jim) has a weekly basketball practice.

Here, Marla doesn't give any course of action whatsoever, but only initiates a thinking process with her son. And their discussion will depend on Mark's view of the situation about his friend Jim's breach of trust. Mark is the one who comes up with possible alternatives on how he sees the problem situation into which his friend has gotten himself. Mark may say something like,

"Well, his parents never let him do such and such things, that's why he had to lie to them," or,

"Well, his parents let his twin brother Seth go with the car to any place he wants, and don't say anything," or even,

"He did a stupid thing, but I think his parents should give him a second chance."

Depending on situations and contexts, parents may want to use requests. A *request* is a demand made on the child with which she *may* or *may not* comply. The course of action is left up to her. Requests can also be either *direct* or *indirect*.

Direct request:

"Would you please set the table, Jack?" Mona asks her fourteen year old son as she's finishing up making dinner.

Indirect request:

"Jack, would you please set the table or should I?"

A distinction must be made here between a request and an *order*. With an order, our youngster doesn't have a choice. Parents give the child clear directives as to what is expected of her.

Order: "Please go brush your teeth now, Sam!"

Here, no alternatives are given to Sam. He doesn't have to think about it as with a request or suggestion. He is going to brush his teeth, and that's that. Orders are intended to bring quick and fast results.

We may be tempted to *mostly* or *only* make orders in most of our interactions with our child since orders bring quick results. As tempting and easy as giving orders to our child can be, this is a recipe for disaster not so far down the road. We can learn to create a much healthier parent-child relationship when we make it possible for our youngster to have a say or make choices. Being civil with a child fosters a much more cooperative attitude while creating a pleasant and positive atmosphere in the home wherein arguments are dealt with mostly through effective and humane persuasion and verbal appeals.

PERSUASION AND VERBAL APPEALS

Emotions are more likely than reason to compel people into action. *Persuasion* appeals to people's emotions. Children's behaviors are motivated much more by their emotions than by reason. A child's *voluntary* compliance to emulate acceptable behaviors is often related to how she feels.

As much as persuasion arouses emotions and gets a child's attention, verbal appeals stress the *benefits* of a particular behavior, thereby motivating her to cooperate in emulating or modifying a particular behavior. The associated benefits of a particular behavior are related to a youngster's desires, wants, needs, and values. To some extent, verbal appeal is similar to persuasion in this regard.

In some situations, it may be difficult or even unwise to try to get a youngster's cooperation through persuasion or verbal appeals. In such a case, *challenging* a child's ego may be an appropriate and effective way to motivate her into cooperation.

CHALLENGING

When a child is capable of doing something, but is not motivated enough to do it, giving her a challenge may be a very effective way to get her into action.

"Is your *inside magic* of making your toys go back into the toy box still working?" Pete asks his three year old son Casey. As Pete somewhat tickles his son Casey's pride, more often than not, Casey will try to prove to his father that, "but of course I can put my toys back into the toy box."

"I'm a big boy," Casey might say, "..and I am very strong and have magic..."

Challenges are important in acquiring new skills, and by the same token boost self-esteem, provided these challenges are not so high that they discourage her, or so low that they don't motivate her enough. Therefore, to be effective, a challenge must be age and skill-appropriate, lest we cause her too much anxiety and hinder her genuine motivation.

"Look what I can do. Gee Mama, this bag of weed is sooo hard to pull. But I can do it, look how I can do it!" shouts five-year-old Josh to his mother, Sally.

"You're right, that's a heavy bag of weed you got there, buddy!" Sally says to her son as she looks at her youngster's contorted face showing how hard he is working. "You are such a big and strong boy, oh my! I am so proud of you!"

A little encouragement can sure go a long way! Children are usually responsive to our appropriate expectations. Everything being equal, high expectations engender high results, and low expectations engender low results. It's as simple as that. Children often can and do surprise their parents when they go looking for challenges on their own initiative. This is usually a by-product of our acknowledging their efforts and accomplishments. Have you ever looked at the face of a two, three, four, or five year old after she succeeds in doing something she's never done before? Like Josh in the above example, for instance.

Young children usually like challenges. And this is critical for their physical and mental growth. Furthermore, this kind of enthusiasm prepares them for further challenges they will have to meet every day when they go to school for instance. A caveat here, as pointed out throughout, is not to confuse genuine challenge and downright nagging, which is counterproductive.

Challenge:

"I don't think you still have your inside-magic to make your dinner-plate go into the sink, Paul? Do you?" works more effectively than the following example.

Nagging:

"Why don't you ever take away your plate and put

it in the sink after you eat, Paul? Do I have to remind you to do that all the time?"

In the above *challenge* example, Paul would most likely get excited to show his mom or dad that he still has his magic. He might, for instance, ask his mother to either close her eyes, turn around, or go out of the room so that he can do his magic, and then surprise her with the results: his plate being in the sink!

With a challenge, we appeal to our youngster's competitive instinct and desire to do better than we expect. In the *nagging* example, the child would most likely feel under attack and therefore become defensive and uncooperative. Another effective approach in getting a child's cooperation, especially with those hormonally challenged adolescents, is making explicit *contracts*.

CONTRACTING

A parent-child contract is a mutual, written or verbal agreement between parent and child. For a parent-child contract to be effective, it must be reasonable, fair, AND feasible. House rules and regulations are but one form of family contract. A contract may include things such as daily chores, respect for other people's property, and acceptable language. Most families have some kind of parent-child contracts, *albeit* implicit. Making these contracts more explicit with clear stipulations of expectations can be a very helpful guidance tool for both parent and child.

The alarming rise of teen drivers' accidents is even more so urgent that we parents need to discuss with our child about rules for her driving privileges, and come up with *written* contract. It is our responsibility to withhold this privilege -- and protect her life and that of others – when she tries to disregard the contract rules. We also need to hold our end of the bargain by coming up with guidelines which eventually motivate her into doing the right thing.

This may sound like an oxymoron, but parents can still resort to *reason*, i.e., an objective analysis of the advantages and disadvantages of situations or events in which their child might find herself. *Reasoning*, especially with our not-yet-balanced adolescent, may seem like walking into a wall and expecting to easily get through! However, by taking the time to discuss and reason with her, it shows the youngster that her parents respect her as an individual, and that her opinions and ideas matter to them even though the choices are hers to make.

CHOICES VS. RESPONSIBILITIES

Children don't often think much about the consequences of their actions, i.e., the possible *future effects* of their choices, until after the fact. They respond to situations according to how they feel at that very moment. We have the task to teach our child from very early on the skills to make acceptable and constructive choices for herself. She must learn that she has a big role to play in her own destiny no matter how she feels at that moment. By making a particular choice, she is also consequently making a choice of a certain result which may or may not turn out to be what she expected in the first place.

Particular choices are linked to *related responsibilities* which are the key to making choices with consequences with which we can live. Two of the different techniques we can teach our child on how to predict possible consequences from choices made are *If-Then* and *Now vs. Later* approaches.

IF-THEN APPROACH

If-then analysis statements can be an effective tool in teaching a child the skills needed to make appropriate and constructive choices. This method may not only help a youngster keep her behavior within certain limits, but may also eventually motivate her into *thinking* about the choices she's about to make. Through this method our adolescent youngster, who may be struggling with the need for immediate gratification, may come to realize that, in most cases, choices are *hers* to make, and therefore the consequences and responsibilities are *hers* to own up to.

We are doing her a disservice when we try to shield her from facing the consequences of her own actions. By making her accountable for her actions, by helping her learn how to pause and think, we are helping her learn about important realities of life. This is, by the way, how she develops *maturity*. The latter doesn't come either naturally or easily. It requires learning specific skills, such as critical thinking, reflecting on past experiences, and being able to live with our choices.

Maturity *never* comes with rescuing, no matter how much we wish it does! It comes with open-mindedness, patience, humility, and sometimes with years of experience. It builds up through life experiences and, at times, from the school of hard knocks. Obviously, our legitimate desire to satisfy our child's needs can go haywire when we focus *mostly* on *short-term* quick fixes rather than *long-term* solutions.

SHORT VS. LONG TERM APPROACH

In the business world, effective leaders always have

plans for their companies' immediate and future activities. These plans have best as well as worst case scenarios for expected AS WELL AS unexpected situations their companies might run into. They prepare themselves for the *unknown*. Being prepared is what makes a difference between a thriving company and a bankrupt one. There is no job under the sun as tough as raising a *responsible* child. Running into problems while doing this job has to be considered as a *given* rather than an unusual event.

As in the business world, we have to be prepared for both the expected and the unexpected. It is impossible to plan ahead for *all* the worst or best case scenarios while raising a responsible child. However, general guidelines, as explained throughout this book, may prove to be helpful.

After a crisis, people usually like to move on quickly with their lives. *Quick fix* solutions to problems seem appealing, particularly *vis-à-vis* problems that demand a lot of emotional involvement and time. As portrayed in the parent-child responsibility chart here below, in her early years, parents have the full bulk of responsibilities vis-à-vis their child. As the child grows older and is taught how to take care of herself, we slowly and steadily let go of micromanaging her daily activities and let her be the person she was born to be.

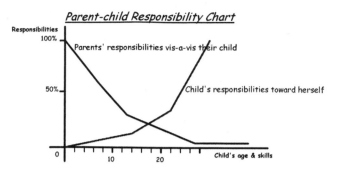

© *Suruba I. Wechsler*

*Everything being equal, as our child grows older
her responsibilities toward herself also go up.
Her parents' responsibilities toward her life and
hers towards herself are inversely related the
older she gets and matures.*

SUMMARY

As their child grows older, parents slowly and steadily make it possible for her to take over her own destiny in life so to speak. To effectively and appropriately pass on the reins, we need to learn the skills that enable us to get our child's cooperation in learning her responsibilities toward herself and her community. Our efforts in getting these appropriate parenting skills make it in turn possible for us to build a stable environment with of a solid foundation for open communication, mutual respect, and a healthy bond among family members.

Regardless of what parenting approach with which we choose to raise our child responsibly, the community in which we live also exerts a tremendous influence in this process so that a parenting approach that may be appropriate and effective in one community may not be appropriate or effective in another. There is, however, one element that is the most influential factor in raising a responsible child: a child usually imitates what the significant persons in her life do.

While most people have plans for their professional lives, many of us, however, don't have any plans on how to approach the toughest profession that we've chosen: being a parent! Fortunately, many parents wind up becoming great parents and role models. "Maternal instinct," as some of us may come to realize, isn't enough to responsibly raise a child into a mature individual. There are, most definitely, some basic parenting skills to be learned. Children are all born uncivilized -- no school of manners where they come from. It's up to us to teach our child how to grow into a mature, confident, compassionate, and responsible adult member of a society.

Let's try to do the best that we can as parents. If we do our "job" as best as we can during our child's first eighteen or so years of life, we will surely be on the road to raising a responsible individual, who will be proud of herself. We, in turn, will be proud of having invested our time and energy during those formative years -- come to think of it, eighteen years or so in our child's life isn't that long in a person's lifetime!

A caution here: we can only try to do the best that we can because trying to be the "perfect" parent or raise the "perfect" child can only bring stress and disappointment for both parent and child. Our child (and us) will make mistakes during this growing process simply because making mistakes is all part of learning, and not cause for either self-pity or blame.

Equally, we also have to go easy on ourselves. Perfect parents don't exist; parents are only too human; they can only seek to do their best and find humane ways to raise their children. We cannot, *all the time,* be very enthusiastic or motivated to parent our child, or loving and supportive for that matter. However, if we put our efforts into doing what is in our child's best interests, *most of the time*, in the not so long run, we will look back and be content that we did do so. We will be glad that we put up with some inconveniences in order to make our parenting responsibility the highest priority. We will be satisfied that we *did* indeed help her grow into a responsible and decent individual. And if our goal has been to be adequate parents, most of the mistakes we make while raising our child will be outweighed by the good, in the long run. Modeling for our child the right thing to do, while providing support based on the interdependence of love AND discipline, is the most powerful parenting approach to a trusting, strong, and honest parent-child relationship.

Index

school/PTA, 38, 45,
79, 154;
social,94, 156
Adapt, 38, 89-90, 124;
-ation; 115;
to environment, 15
Adequacy;
inadequacy, 65-66,
92, 105
Adequate;
adequately, 29, 37,
44, 132;
inadequately, 65-66,
92, 105, 143;
parent, viii, ix, 1,3-
6,11, 43, 45-46, 48,
69, 84, 141, 143, 177
Adjustments, 104, 123;
re- 104, 136
Adolescence, 12, 39-
40, 44, 56, 70, 85,
88, 101, 104, 110,
136, 139, 143-144,
157, 161, 164;
adolescents, 2, 6, 19,
27, 40, 42-43, 55,
56-59, 61, 119, 121-
122, 124, 136-141,
143-144, 147-148,
151, 160-162, 171,
173
Adoption, 3, 6, 10
Adulthood, 39-40, 88,
137;

adults, 5, 33, 57-58,
87, 106, 119, 140,
150, 157, 164
Advertisement, 42-43
Advice, 2, 42, 61, 125,
138, 144
Affection, 12-13, 30,
91, 93, 141
Affinity, 1
Affirmation, 99
Africa, 9, 153
Age, 5, 9, 19, 21, 23,
30, 36-37, 47, 59,
68, 70, 94-95, 99,
104, 115-116, 118,
121-122, 127, 134,
145, 153-154, 160,
162, 170;
school, 90
Agreement, 4-5, 97,
171
Ailing, 23
Alcohol, 84, 101,157,
161-162
Allowance, 103, 162
Alternatives, 27, 31-
32, 35, 77, 81, 166,
168
Ambiguous, 90, 92,
157
Anchor, 40;
family, 139
Angels, 3
Anger, 54-55, 57-58,

141

Gratification, 41, 43, 57, 87, 137, 173

Ground, 93, 111, 167;
back-, 93;
-ing, 145, 148;
play-, 121

Growth, 14, 32, 39-40, 65, 170

Guarantee, 33, 36, 89, 97, 108

Guidance, ix, 6, 15, 37, 40-41, 43, 119, 137, 144, 172

Guilt, 44, 65, 105-106, 134;
-y, 17, 80

H

Habits, 92, 99, 115, 121, 135, 153

Hadassah, 83

Handicap, 5, 45, 60, 90, 105, 158

Hands, 28, 34, 55, 76, 91, 111, 121;
-off, 63

Happy, viii, ix, 7, 12, 14, 27, 44, 46, 51, 71, 79, 95, 127;
-ily, 5;
un-, 47, 51

Hard knocks, 138, 145, 174

Harmony, 5, 11, 150

Hate, 10, 48, 56, 138

Health, 13, 118;
-ier, 168;
un-, 11, 107;
-y, 13, 28-29, 45, 52-53, 55-56, 60, 65, 73-74, 82, 86, 94, 98, 105-106, 118, 120-121, 144-146, 149, 175

Hearing, 153

Home, 19, 26, 36-37, 39, 45, 51, 55, 68, 70, 75, 77, 80, 82, 89-90, 93-94, 115-116, 123-124, 129, 132-133, 148, 153, 156-160, 168;
foster, 68;
stay-at-, 23, 43

Honest, 20, 22, 27-28, 69, 72, 141, 177;
dis-, 28;
-ly, 7, 17;
-y, 22-24, 41, 79, 81, 160

Honeymoon, 121

Hope, 7, 25, 56, 65-66, 112;
-fully, 56

Hormone, 160;
-ally challenged, 40, 55, 85, 143, 171

level of, 21

Intentions, viii, 27, 44, 65, 69, 75, 105, 109, 119, 122

Interact, 13, 15, 17, 20, 31, 38, 40, 45, 54, 66, 73, 90-91, 97, 127, 133-134, 163;
-ing, 1, 31, 65;
-ion, 7, 13, 16, 19-20, 26, 32-33, 36, 57, 65, 85, 107, 118, 120, 123, 127, 135, 149, 168;
-ive, 31, 45

Interest, 2, 8, 10-11, 17, 20, 23, 32, 35, 63, 71-73, 75, 79, 91-92, 103, 114, 133, 154, 161, 177;
-ing, 44;
non-, 6, 13

Interfaith, *see* couple

Intervention, 112, 119;
professional, 92

Intimidation, 92

Invest, 5, 10, 47, 176;
-ing, 92;
-ment, 19

Involve, viii, 3-5, 31-32, 37-38, 60-61, 65, 67, 153;
-ing, 92;
-ment, 174

Issues, 4-5, 21, 58, 63, 122-124, 141, 157;
conflicting, 41, 57;
Drugs/ alcohol/ sex, 84, 101, 161;
personality, 134

J

Journey, 5;
adulthood, 39;
life, 47;
parenting, 105

Joy, 2, 30, 54, 107;
en-, 88, 119, 154

Judgment, 42, 101, 109, 116-117

Justify, 21

K

Knack, 11

L

Laisser-faire, 44, 86

Language, 32, 85, 98, 171;
Abusive/ foul, 57, 85, 117;
body, 17, 55

Lax, 9, 62-63

Learning, viii, 3, 10, 13-14, 26-27, 35, 45, 53, 57-58, 61, 68, 72-73, 80, 82, 92-93, 96, 102, 104, 116, 121,

family, 96, 121

Memories, 1;
see also childhood

Message, 35, 71, 81, 89, 144

Mind, 2, 16-17, 23, 27, 50, 58, 69-70, 103-104, 106, 128, 135, 150;
state of, 58, 124, 139

Miracles, 99

Mirage, 3

Mistakes, viii, 14-15, 33, 42, 63, 65, 69, 77-79, 89, 105, 122, 141, 177

Modeling, ix, 84, 177

Moderation, 52, 99, 139

Modification, 104;
see also behavior

Molesters, 157

Money, 103, 113, 147-148, 156, 162, 166-167

Mood, 47, 58, 95, 154, 163

Morale, 140

Mother, 6-8, 11, 20, 22-23, 41, 48-51, 60-61, 66-68, 82, 85, 100, 110-112, 114, 117, 121-122, 130, 132, 140, 142, 147-148, 158-159, 170-171;
nature, 41, 60-61, 86;
grand-, 22;
-in-law, 23;
step-, 34

Motivation, 65, 67, 79, 92, 170

Motives, 7

Myths, 136

N

Nagging, 95, 139, 155, 164, 171

Natural, 11, 24, 57, 73;
-ly, 14, 19, 25, 39, 60-61, 118, 162-163, 173;
see also consequences

Needs, 2, 4, 10, 13, 21, 25, 30, 35, 37, 40-42, 47, 53-54, 61, 69, 75, 77, 86, 90, 94, 98-99, 101, 104, 108, 125-127, 132-134, 137, 139-141, 144, 151, 154, 162-163, 169, 174

Negligence, 44

Neighbors, 11

Nephew, 20, 59, 123

Newborn, 11, 13

News, ix, 20-21, 23, 67, 84, 114, 137

Niece, 20, 59, 142-143
Notion, 3, 24, 36, 73, 90
Nurse, 21-22, 116-117
Nurturing, 13-14, 24;
environment, 29

O

Obedience, 26, 66, 140;
blind, 26;
dis-, 85, 141
Objection, 1, 125
Obligation, 27, 95, 133, 162
Observation, viii, x
Obstacles, 42
Officer, 152
Offspring, ix
Opportunity, 25, 32, 41, 48, 78, 141, 149;
-ies, 16, 73, 77
Optimistic, 13
Orders,16, 86, 165, 168
Organizational. 153
Out there, ix, 1, 24, 27, 30, 88, 157-158
Outlook, 67, 92
Overindulgent, 91
Overloading, 160
Oxymoron, 15, 172

P

Package, 93, 118
Pain, 22, 35, 42, 106-107, 149;
-ful, 60
Paraphrasing, 131
Parent, ii, viii, ix, x, 1-15, 17-48, 50-52, 54, 56-73, 75-81, 83-96, 100, 103, 105-109, 112-113, 115, 117-118, 120, 122, 125-128, 132, 134-141, 143-147, 149-151, 153-154, 156, 158, 160-164, 167-168, 170-172, 174-177;
-al, 15, 33, 43-44, 72, 85-87, 96, 107, 136, 162;
-ing, viii, ix, 1-4, 6, 8-10, 12, 27, 48, 56, 61, 64-65, 67-69, 71, 81, 86, 92,104-105, 109, 112, 122, 138, 156, 175, 177
Participation, 25, 32, 43, 60, 124, 155, 157
Particular, ix, 4, 8, 28, 37-38, 61, 64, 69, 85, 88, 94, 96, 104, 110, 121, 149, 163, 169, 173;
-ities, 85;

88, 92, 110, 115, 117,
121, 124, 138-139,
143, 149, 153, 160,
163-165, 172;
-ground, 121;
-ing, 70, 106, 116,
129, 131, 145
Polite, 16, 123;
-ness, 63-64
Position, 5-6, 33, 35,
38, 46, 48, 59, 64, 89,
99, 109, 119, 138,
145, 150, 161;
dis-, 5, 24, 30, 124
Possessive, 36
Potential, 3, 8, 24, 38,
47, 62, 118, 156
Power, 4, 24, 26-27,
29, 43, 59, 85-86, 91,
118, 145;
-ful, 79, 99, 120, 155,
164, 177;
-less, 130;
will-, 113
Practice, ix, 59, 122,
167
Praise, 79, 101-102,
146
Preach, ix
Predict, 12, 88, 173;
-able, 94;
-ability, 95;
un-able, 118
Predispose, 164;

-ing, 163
Pre-logic, *see* logic
Prerequisites, 85, 163
Prevent, 106, 121;
-ing, 120;
-ive, 115
Pride, 2, 83, 107, 155-
156, 169
Primary, ix;
caregivers, 8, 13, 37-
38, 141
Privilege, 88, 145, 148,
172
Problem(s), 4, 7, 20,
22-23, 29, 33, 35, 38,
55-66, 68-69, 72, 74,
77, 91-92, 97-98,
107-108, 114, 118,
120-121, 123-124,
126, 131, 133-135,
141, 143, 149-151,
167, 174;
-atic, 7, 144;
behavior, 107;
childhood, 66;
family, 22, 77;
marital, 4;
personal, 22, 107;
psychological, 65;
school, 38
Process, 4, 7, 14, 33,
77, 80-82, 84, 99,
141, 157, 166-167,
176-177;

106, 113, 117, 166,
168, 170-171, 173;
-ing, 85
Revolutionary, 152
Reward, 3, 26, 73,
102-104;
immaterial, 103;
-ing, 5, 64, 102, 146,
163;
material, 103, 156
Rights, 119
Rituals, 31,136
Role, ix, 13, 25, 29, 56,
77, 82, 85-87, 90, 94,
124, 138-139, 143,
151, 163, 172;
model, 3, 41, 43, 57-
58, 82, 84-85, 119,
137, 176
Root, 4, 92, 118
Routine, 68, 94-96, 99,
146, 153-154, 156,
165;
-ly, 94
Rules, 2, 15, 62, 70-71,
73-74, 84, 87, 89-90,
92-93, 95-97, 108,
115, 119, 121, 125,
133, 146, 163, 172;
contract, 172;
family, 85, 90, 95-96,
104, 107, 120-121,
133, 141, 162;
house, 73, 87, 92, 95-

96, 98, 121, 124, 171;
school, 37, 133

S
Safety, 72, 115-116,
138, 165
Schedule, 3, 98; over-
ed, 99
School, 8, 24, 26, 28,
31-32, 36-39, 45, 68,
70-71, 75-76, 79-80,
90, 110, 116, 132-
133, 135, 138, 145,
147, 154, 162, 170,
174, 176;
nursery, 117;
pre-, 36, 45
Security, 89, 98;
in-, 8, 44, 57, 90, 130
Seeds, 12
Seeing, 153, 155
Self-analysis, *see*
analysis
Self-centered, 118
Self-control, *see* control
Self-defeating, 9
Self-discipline, *see* discipline
Self-esteem, ix, 15, 18,
24, 26, 66, 70, 81-82,
101, 106, 136, 143,
151, 155-156, 170
Self-reliant, 26

Printed in the United States
39877LVS00001B/31